AN INTRODUCTION TO
ARWROLOGY

Courtesy of Canadian Army Photo

Dedicated to Fighters for World Freedom

urtesy of Public Information . National Film Board Photographs.

ARWROLOGY

By
GORDON E. PERRIGARD, M.D.

RENOUF PUBLISHING CO.
MONTREAL

PUBLISHER'S NOTE

This reprint edition of *Arwrology,* Gordon Perrigard's classic book of World War II-era hand-to-hand combat, is published with the permission of the original Canadian publisher, Renouf Publishing Company. Visit its Web site at www.renoufbooks.com.

Arwrology
by Gordon E. Perrigard, M.D.

Copyright ©, Canada, 1943 by Gordon E. Perrigard, M.D.

Reprint edition published 2006 by Paladin Press

ISBN 13: 978-1-58160-507-5
Printed in the United States of America

Published by Paladin Press, a division of
Paladin Enterprises, Inc.
Gunbarrel Tech Center
7077 Winchester Circle
Boulder, Colorado 80301 USA
+1.303.443.7250

Direct inquiries and/or orders to the above address.

PALADIN, PALADIN PRESS, and the "horse head" design are trademarks belonging to Paladin Enterprises and registered in United States Patent and Trademark Office.

All rights reserved. Except for use in a review, no portion of this book may be reproduced in any form without the express written permission of the publisher.

Neither the author nor the publisher assumes any responsibility for the use or misuse of information contained in this book.

Visit our Web site at www.paladin-press.com

PREFACE

VICTORY in modern war demands scientific knowledge. There is need in war time for a text book which gives more than miscellaneous, incommensurate directions on how you might throw a man to the ground, break his hold, stamp on his toes, grab his testicles or push your fingers into his eyes. In the All-Out Hand-to-Hand Fighting methods of Arwrology, medical science has contributed a deadly efficiency never before attained.

Co-ordinated, organized group instruction is required.

No book can teach everything in any subject and a false sense of security is likely to arise if that impression is accepted. This is the first of a series of volumes which will teach a technique of fighting in which every movement learned helps to reinforce the next one learned. The actions are easily co-ordinated. This book is not a miscellaneous collection of holds but a definite foundation. It is the beginning of an organized course in hand-to-hand fighting, which can be carried on to three thousand methods. The methods are designed so that a new, simple and effective method of group instruction may be easily carried out.

Positive form of exercise with emotional reinforcement.

The Associate Professor of Psychology at McGill University, Dr. C. E. Kellogg, asserts that Arwrology gives a positive form of exercise which is a normal form of motivation. You produce movements which you know are specifically designed for use in fighting.

Arwrology has *"emotional reinforcement"*, and in this way differs from the usual prescribed setting up exercises. If you are thinking about what you want to get done, instead of yourself, you will accomplish the result better and develop yourself better.

It is like the centipede which wanted to cross a road, and asked with incertitude :

"Pray, which foot comes after which?"

After vainly trying to figure it out, the poor centipede finally dropped prostrated in the ditch, not able to go in any direction.

We get better results in work if we keep strongly in mind what we want to accomplish eventually.

Develop conditioned reflexes for fighting

Exercise should be designed to quicken "fighting" reflexes so that correct "fighting" reactions will become automatic. The exercise motions should have a conterminous relationship with the motions to be used in actual fighting, when such a contingency arises. The muscular development will generally look after itself.

The oppressing excitement of being under fire may in occasional cases cause a soldier to forget the methods of unarmed combat which have been taught him, unless special care has been taken to develop the methods almost into conditioned reflexes. The psycho-physical calisthenics described here, such as one man throwing up to a hundred men one after the other in quick succession, develop conditioned reflexes for actual fighting under strain.

EPITOME

This book is an attempt to start you on the study of Arwrology, a scientific method of all-out hand-to-hand fighting. It will enable you to overcome opponents who are larger and stronger than yourself.

I have included some *conditioning exercises* which may be practised anywhere. You are given the technique of *Blow Power* to knock out your opponents. Certain simple fundamental *throws, holds* and *defence movements* are described. With this knowledge you will be able to build up your efficiency in fighting.

A few *death locks* are described. Be careful when practising these. You are given several simple methods of defence against a man armed with a revolver. Most of the fighting methods mentioned are designed so that a defensive movement is carried further into an offensive one.

A portion of the book is devoted to the *use of a dagger* and to the *defence against a dagger,* since this important aspect of hand-to-hand fighting can easily be neglected in the general training of the armed forces.

* * *

Why should *you* study Arwrology? If you are in the active armed forces, the answer is clear. You will know superior fighting methods than your enemy when it comes to hand-to-hand conflict. What you may lack in size or strength can be compensated by your knowledge of Arwrology. Even though you are outnumbered, with a knowledge of Arwrology, you will still have a good fighting chance. It will give you grim confidence in yourself.

If you are in the "Reserve", Veteran Guards,

"C.P.C." or similar organizations, it will help to harden up any "arm-chair" muscles you have, and if the enemy is ever encountered, it will make you a killer. That's not a gentle thought, but we are in warring times. Self-preservation is a strong sentiment. Who knows when the alternative of kill or be killed will be forced upon any of us. We fight for life and the four freedoms for the world.

If you are physically weak, Arwrology will enable you to use every ounce of strength that you possess with the greatest possible effect in your fight.

If you are a woman, in uniform or not, some of these methods may be of service to you, especially in times of blackouts, night shifts in factories and increasing thuggings and cases of assault.

Whoever you are, *someday this book may save your life.*

INTRODUCTION

I

IN Arwrology one attempts to do the unexpected, quickly, accurately. It is a science based on some understanding of neuro-vascular anatomy and physiology, using balance and leverage to the best advantage.

For many years the most intimate details of the science and art of hand-to-hand fighting have been analyzed by the Society of Arwrologists. With meticulous anatomical care, various techniques have been dissected and reconstructed into a comparatively new science called "Arwrology", derived from the old Welsh word Arwr, meaning a Hero, an All-Out Hand-To-Hand Fighter. Created from a medical background, it frequently has the corresponding nomenclature and explanations.

GREAT STRENGTH IS NOT REQUIRED

Arwrology does not need to have the prerequisite of a powerful physique, usually associated with boxing, wrestling or other sports.

Thus a captured soldier whose strength has been sapped, whose senses have been obfuscated by lack of sleep, or whose vitality has been vitiated by poor food or germane causes, may still be strong enough to overcome his guards and effect his freedom.

Thus a wounded soldier may still have enough strength to employ its methods for his own defence.

The psycho-physical calisthenics of this science can develop individual groups of muscles to an extraordinary degree of efficiency and it can give the student a specialized neuro-muscular co-ordination so necessary in unarmed combat.

II

Psychological Aspect

One of the main features is psychological. It gives a man a feeling of self-confidence. Like an imaginary gun at his belt, it is always ready to assist him when he tries "to do the right as he sees the right".

Psychology has been applied to war in vocational guidance by personnel corps, in placing men to best advantage. It is imperative that a man should be placed in the army where his abilities or training can be utilized to the greatest advantage.

Although a soldier may have ability, he must have also a conviction of his own power. Basic training should be so designed as to instill in him a sense of resourcefulness, of superb fearlessness in individual combat. If he knows from his training that he can overcome four men, then he will be able to project and sublimate this feeling of confidence into whatever mechanized instrument of war he is employing.

* * *

Beat them at their own game

Let us not underestimate our foes. That would be almost crassitude. Many of the Japanese, through training, have attained remarkable self-confidence. Some of the men in the Ishikawajima, the two-man tankettes, and in the two-man submarines have such confidence in themselves that if they do not vanquish their enemy, they consider themselves disgraced and candidates for suicide. (Sepukku)

What can be done with such people? You have to beat them at their own game!

WIDE INTEREST IN ARWROLOGY

For over ten years, I have observed the acquisition of self-reliance, initiative and general fearlessness in many graduates of the Society of Arwrologists, whose members represent a cross section of society, chosen from practically every profession.

The medical profession is represented by professors of anatomy and surgery, specialists and general practitioners. Members and executives of the Royal Canadian Mounted Police, the Provincial Police, the Canadian National Railway Police and other police forces have been accepted. In the armed forces, members are drawn from all ranks. Civilian members include prominent scientists of the National Research Council of Canada, and elsewhere, presidents and employees of some of the largest industrial concerns, and university instructors and students. High nobility is also represented.

Why is there such a varied interest in Arwrology? Why do so many different types of men study it as a hobby? Is there some hidden desire for security from aggression by force? I am inclined to think so. Once this sense of security is obtained, better work can be done in any field.

In time of war, the non-professional soldier has to be weaned from his civil life values and in a short time he must attain an aggressive maturity along military lines. He must be able to consider himself invincible in some form or other. He needs confidence in personal combat regardless of his size.

Individualism is important

Many of our foes have an implacable idea that their army, airforce or navy is invincible, but when left on their own, personally, they may know how to follow, but not how to lead, even themselves sometimes. They are frequently confused and puzzled, unable to cope with the conflicts of an environment thrown solely against them. Here we can build up an advantage by a training which will help the development of individualism. A study of Arwrology could aid this, and not inadvertently.

Revisions suggested in army physical training

The four "Nelsonic" principles of Admiral Lord Fisher of Kilverstone for winning a war are said to have been (1) Self-reliance (2) Fearlessness of responsibility (3) Fertility of resource, and (4) Power of initiative.

Without being carping and too opprobrious, I would like to suggest that some revisions of physical training as it is practised to-day are necessary to underline these ideas. Many of the present methods are incommensurate with the needs. Often old smug institutionalized methods of instruction have adherents, generally of the gerontocracy class, whose sclerosed intellect eclipses their vision. They become negationists, refusing to abrogate out-moded customs.

I do not wish to write interminably about this, but under such a system, archaic methods of physical training which are not pragmatic can act in an astringent manner by drying up the freshness of modern troops. Arwrology is of use here. It can help in developing an accipitral zeal for seeking the enemy·

The start of "P.T." is good from the aspect that it does fit a man out with a reasonable standard of health. The lack which may be pointed out is one of purposefulness. While learning the routine exercises, it could be shown how to put good physical condition to advantage, by teaching Arwrology. In this science, all exercise has the avowed purpose of making each individual, even the agnothic type, an excellent fighting unit, with or without weapons. Thus, an important factor is added to useful, enjoyable exercise. This factor is "Self-Confidence". Psychologically, it is very important for any member of the Armed Forces to feel capable of handling all situations where physical contact with the enemy is at hand.

Though death is more "mechanized" than ever before, it should be realized that it is the individual behind the machine who must show superiority in the final assay. Self-reliance must be developed as well as technical skill. Mental attitude is very important, and Arwrology can be a cure for Gremlin-phobia.

Army calisthenics

Regarding army calisthenics, we should abrogate a lot of the hands up, hands in every direction "P.T." exercises as absonant. Instead of the knee bending with arms up, arms forward, arms sideways and then arms

---

In Commando work especially, Arwrology could work like an arrow in the dark.
Captain W. Aalto, XIV Guerrilla Corps, Spanish Republican army, said in a letter to me:
"For swift, silent work at the proper time, it is of course invaluable."

down exercises, teach the Arwrology upward thrusts of the arms, which the soldiers and students should be told, may reach up with trained accuracy and speed into the neck of a Nazi, some night in the jungle or concentration camp.

Teach the powerful "T-D" forward thrusts of the Arwrology D-U-R-A throws which some day may hurl an amazed and permanently dazed Japanese over the head of a Commando.

Teach the edge-hand blows which, against the carotid sinus in the neck of any Nazi ally, will help to silence his vocal cords forever. Never teach "Hands up", or "Arms down."

Silent, crawling exercises in assault positions could do more to stimulate circulation, imagination and fighting ambition that all the "Ceremonial Drill" ever used to fill in time.

Whoever heard of soldiers practicing "Ceremonial Drill" in their spare time? "Ceremonial Drill" and "Spare Time" have a definite celibate relationship. But Arwrology practice could act like some missing emotional vitamin in maintaining esprit de corps. It has the play element, so valuable in times of nervous strain. The practice of Arwrology could remove a bored soldier from the nadir of depression to the zenith of zeal. It could be continued by the men when off duty in desert, on ship, or in barracks, and the physical and morale conditioning would not stop when the specified short training time has elapsed.

Arwrology is the improved bitter medicine to treat the enemy with in hand-to-hand fighting.

The old and comparatively weaker medicines of Jiu-Jitsu, Judo, boxing and wrestling are periodically rechristened with new names, each one of which reminds me of Byron's "Gilded halo hovering round decay."

Arwrology is not only a new word, it is a new, improved science of combat. This fact will be appreciated the more it is studied.

Some boxing, wrestling, unarmed combat, defendu, Jiu-Jitsu, Judo, Tan-Jitsu, Taku-Jitsu and many other methods have been taught to members of the fighting forces already. That is fine. The more the better. All knowledge is not new, but much quietly becomes obsolescent. It is high time that all these old miscellaneous bits of teaching were objectively evaluated, and the few effective methods incorporated into one master programme for teaching all-out hand-to-hand fighting methods.

The advanced knowledge of Arwrology can add more to the training curricula now being used. It should be incorporated or substituted since it includes the best methods of the fighting arts.

As explained in a requested lecture to McGill University students, some of the purposes of Arwrology are to assist the individual to maintain his right of self-preservation, to develop his physique and general health, and to enable him, regardless of physical handicaps, to do the right as he sees the right.

At a lecture to the Duke of Connaught 6th Royal Canadian Hussars, several methods of Arwrology applicable to war work were shown. The enthusiasm of the men for such training was high. Desire has been evidenced among military units for such instruction, as shown following lectures to the armed forces by members of the Society.

As believed by a well-known member of the Society, the late Colonel E. M. Renouf, the methods of instruction should be facilitated by simple text books. This is the first of such a series.

In the usual classes of the Society of Arwrologists, after a student's membership application has been accepted, he is started on a series of hardening exercises which include methods of striking an opponent with everything from the edge of his hand to the heels of his feet, Blow Power. Then come the endless interlocking sequences of paralyzing nerve grips, bone twisting and dislocating locks, vindictive throws and the silent, death-dealing Arwr locks.

The student learns how to hurl four or more of his comrades consecutively through the air in almost as short a time as it takes him to grab them, and, especially if he has had an inferiority complex, he gradually develops a confidence in himself which assures him that he need not kneel to anyone through domination by force. He feels freedom. He can project this feeling into all his endeavours. The psychological effect is remarkable, even with the opsimath, and permeates with strength every future conflict and problem. He is elated with the illation that he can be equal to his task.

The psychological effect of possessing a working knowledge of Arwrology is bound to give soldier and civilian alike, a sense of security which in turn will help to foster in him initiative, fearlessness and self-confidence.

Arwrology will help to develop the self-confidence so necessary before persistence, determination and the ambition to use every faculty and resource can be pushed to ultimate limits.

In this book and the volumes to follow, I shall attempt to explain some of the methods outlined above as taught in the Society.

ARWROLOGY—LIKE THE ENDLESS KNOT

The beauty of Arwrology is that nearly all the methods can interlock with each other or reinforce each other. So that if one method happens to fail, another should be ready for just such emergency, Arwrology is a rhythmical science, with interlocking holds, and follow-up methods. As your knowledge of the art progresses, your actions become more rhythmical, deadly and automatic.

III

ARWROLOGY IS A DEATH TRAP OF WHICH THE STUDENT BECOMES THE MASTER

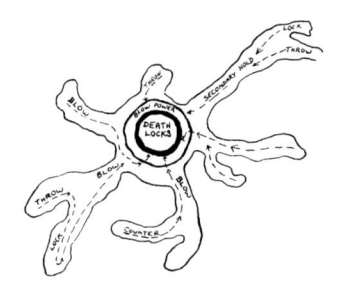

Fig. 2

Arwrology is a living trap. A suitable but rather abstruse comparison would be the amoeba.

The amoeba is a small organism, having a nucleus at its centre. Around this is another portion called the peri-nucleus. Outside of these two, there is a soft, liquid-like substance, forming the pseudopodia, which move about, snaring objects, drawing them in toward the peri-nucleus and finally the nucleus,—like the arms of an octapus.

XIII

In Arwrology, the most important holds are the death dealing "Arwr" locks. They form the nucleus of the science.

Second in importance are the blows and kicks, many of which are fatal, and they form an accretion around the "Arwr" locks, comparable to the perinucleus of the amoeba.

The rest of the science includes nerve grips, throws and locks. They are like the pseudopodia of the amoeba, feeding the deadly centre. They are designed to lead the opponent into positions for receiving the death blows or the death locks.

* * *

Before you Start

1. *Be Too Careful.* Too much emphasis cannot be placed on care when practising the methods which follow. Great strength is not a prerequisite for this science. Necks and hearts may be broken easily by premature enthusiasm or horseplay.

2. *Two Taps.* Two light taps anywhere by you or your partner demand IMMEDIATE release from any hold.

3. *Know Both Sides* (K.B.S.) After learning a method using either the right or left side of your body, practise the same method again, using the other side.

4. *Does It Work?* Be sceptical. Do not trust every hold you have read about or have seen. Try it yourself, on *different* people. Put it to a test. If you find that some of these methods do not work as well as expected, it may be that you have misunderstood some important point. Read the instructions again. The method may not be suitable for your size, weight and development. Slight variations may be necessary. Not

all stereotyped methods are fool-proof; but they can contribute something to your aggregate knowledge of hand-to-hand fighting.

    5. *Individual Differences.* Because of the differences in size, weight and strength, among students and opponents, slight variations may be used, governed by the individual need. Practise the tricks against many partners. Employ group practice. Experiment with all methods, adding little points to suit your particular physique and ability.

CONTENTS

Dedicated to Fighters for World Freedom . . . . Frontispiece
Speed is very important . . . . Following frontispiece

                                                                                                          Page

PREFACE   I

    Co-ordinated, organized group instruction is required. Positive form of exercise with emotional reinforcement. Develop conditioned reflexes for fighting. Epitome.

INTRODUCTION   V

    I. Great strength is not required. II. Psychological aspect. Beat them at their own game. Wide interest in Arwrology. Individualism is important. Revisions suggested in army physical training. Army calisthenics. III. Arwrology is a death trap of which the student becomes the master. Before you start.

PART I

PSYCHO-PHYSICAL CALISTHENICS AND HARDENING EXERCISES

Chapter   Page

1. – HOW TO CRAWL 1
    The Silent Semi-Crawl 2
    What To Do, If 7
    Miscellaneous Points 11
2. – INTRODUCTION 15
    Why? 15
    Anything Can Happen If You Do Not Know How To Fall Without Injury 18
    How? 22
        1. How to fall without injury 23
        2. How to rise up from a sitting position without using the hands 28
            1. The "Straight Rise Up" Exercise 28
            2. The "Spin To The Feet" Exercise 30
    Preparative Exercises 34
3. – KNEE-BLOW PSYCHO-PHYSICAL CALISTHENICS . . . 39
    For One To A Thousand Men 39
    Psychological Aspect 41
4. -- UNARMED "BLOW POWER" 43
    The back of your elbow 44
    The little finger edge of your hand 46
    Edge-hand blow exercise 47
    Your fist. Stiff finger tips. Base of palm. 50
    Front of elbow. Knee. Kicks with your toe. Kicks with your heel. Helmet. 51
    1. Back-elbow and edge-hand blow calisthenics with a partner 52
    2. 'Blow Power' practice with a sand-bag 55

Chapter	Page
Some General Points	56

Forward crouch. "Crouch Walk" exercise. "Jumping Attack" exercise. Your neck. For marching soldiers. Abdominal muscles. Position of your feet. Keep close. Keep moving. Direction of blows. Reaction time. Try these. Spinning.

Kicking Practice	63
5. — THE D-U-R-A HOLD	69

1. Exercise. 2. Psychological Value
3. Method of Carrying a Wounded Man with one Hand.

4. Offense Throw.	69
How To Learn The D-U-R-A Hold	71
Anatomical Explanation of the "T-D" Grip	72
One Man Against Four D-U-R-A Throw Psycho-Physical Calisthenics	76
Miscellaneous Methods	79

PART II
ATTACK METHODS

1. — ASSAULT TRIP THROW

(Attacking below the arms)	83
Attacking his left side	83
Tips To Make The Throw Easier When Attacking His Left Side	86
Attacking His Right Side	91

2. — STEP BACK TRIP THROW

(Attacking above the arms)	95
Speed Throw	99

DEATH LOCKS

3. — NECK ROPE THROW	103
Tips on the "Neck Rope Throw"	106
4. — THE POSTERIOR ARWR LOCK	111
Extra points	120
5. — CAROTID ARTERY ARWR LOCK	123
In actual combat	126

PART III
AGAINST A GUN

1. — DEFENCE AGAINST A GUN HELD IN FRONT OF YOU WHEN YOUR ARMS ARE UP	135
2. — DEFENCE AGAINST A GUN HELD IN FRONT OF YOU WHEN YOUR ARMS ARE DOWN	139
3. — DEFENCE-OFFENSE MOVEMENT AGAINST A GUN HELD AGAINST THE BACK OF YOUR NECK	141
4. — DEFENCE-OFFENSE MOVEMENT AGAINST A GUN POINTED AT YOUR BACK	147
Discussion	151

PART IV
THE DAGGER

Chapter	Page
The "Arwr" Dagger	155
1. – HOW TO ATTACK WITH A COMMANDO DAGGER	
The Left Elbow Lead	157
Surface Anatomy	159
"En Passant"	161
2. – HOW TO USE A DAGGER	

In the following six movements, you hold the dagger in your right hand.

No. 1
Defence-Offense Movement Against A Two Hand Downward Grip On Your Right Wrist 163

No. 2
"Defence-Offense Movement With Blows" Against A Right Hand Downward Grip On Your Right Wrist 166

No. 3
"Snap Off" Defence-Offense Movement Against A Right Hand Downward Grip On Your Right Wrist 172

No. 4
Defence-Offense Movement Against A Left Hand Downward Grip On Your Right Wrist 175

No. 5
"Elbow Swing" Defence-Offense Movement Against A "Right" Hand Upward Grip On Your Right Wrist 179

No. 6
"Elbow Swing" Defence-Offense Movement Against A "Left" Hand Upward Grip On Your Right Wrist 181

3. – THE DAGGER OF THE ENEMY
HOW TO AVOID IT

In the following five movements your enemy holds a dagger in his right hand. You are unarmed.

No. 1
The "Two-Hand Twist" Defence-Offense Movement Against An Upward Thrust 185

No. 2
The Left Hand Grip "Roll" Defence Against An Upward Thrust
   How to flip a knife out of an opponent's hand 189
   General Rule 190
   How to flip a club out of an opponent's hand 194

No. 3
Arm-Lock Defence Against An Upward Thrust 198

No. 4
"Arm About Twist" Defence Against A Downward Thrust 202

No. 5
Arm-Lock Defence Against a Downward Jab 205

4. – BAYONET THRUST DEFENCE-OFFENSE MOVEMENT 209
A Simple and Effective Method 215

PART V

Chapter	Page
1. — STRANGLE HOLD DEFENCE	217
"Tips" on Strangle Hold Defence	222
Adaptation to Military Psycho-Physical Calisthenics	226
2. — THE ANKLE CLAMP THROWS	
1. (a) Face Forward, From his *Left* Side	227
(b) Face Forward, From his *Right* Side	228
2. (a) Head Back, From his *Left* Side	233
(b) Head Back, From his *Right* Side	234
Ankle Clamp Throw Psycho-Physical Calisthenics for the Armed Forces	235
3. — DEFENCE-OFFENSE MOVEMENTS AGAINST A GRIP ON YOUR WRIST	239
Other Methods	242
Defence-Offense With Blows Against A Grip On Your Wrist	243
4. — SEVERAL SIMPLE TRICKS	
No. 1	
Bend Back Finger	247
No. 2	
Push In Knee	248
No. 3	
Head Twist	249
No. 4	
Foot Twist	250
No. 5	
Wrist Bend	251
No. 6	
An Empty Gun Used As A Weapon	252
No. 7	
Push In Knee	253
No. 8	
"Spin Under" Escape From Arm-Lock	254
Points To Remember	255
What About Your Weight	256
How to gain weight	256
How to loose weight	257
R-OLOGY	261
Acknowledgment	263

Over 225 Illustrations

For authentic reports of actual cases where Arwrology has been applied see pages 12, 27, 45, 49, 50, 56, 71, 93 and 130.

Speed is very important

If anyone can see what you are doing,
you are doing it too slowly!

(*Photograph of author taken at 1/300 second
during Paramount Motion Picture "Judo Expert"*)

PART I

PSYCHO-PHYSICAL CALISTHENICS AND HARDENING EXERCISES

Chapter 1

HOW TO CRAWL

CRAWLING is a strengthening exercise. In fact it is one of the first that we indulge in. So I thought it would be an elementary way to commence a series of hardening exercises for All-Out Hand-to-Hand Fighters, Arwr-Men.

To teach you how to crawl implies that there is more than one way for a soldier or guerilla to crawl forward.

There is the "Down on All Fours" and generally "Up in Behind" method (Fig. 3). One fault with most crawlers is that they keep their rear up too high. A second point is that they make too much noise.

If carrying a rifle and crawling on your left side, one good way is to grab the muzzle with your right hand and keep the butt resting on your left thigh. This is the "Side Crawl", which is good, but slow, and often noisy (Fig. 4).

One method is suggested, the Silent Semi-Crawl. It will be described in detail. In actual combat conditions, the soldier should suit the crawl position to the terrain, visibility and immediate action.

← KEEP IT LOW

Fig. 3
The "Down on All Fours" and generally "Up in Behind" method of crawling.

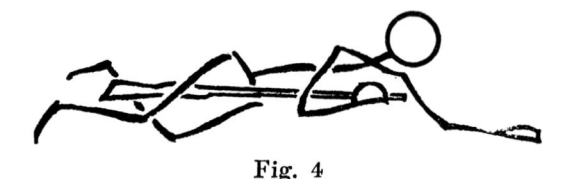

Fig. 4
Side Crawl With Rifle.

THE SILENT SEMI-CRAWL

This method, like all others has faults, but something valuable may be gained by its practice besides a 'house-maid's knee.'

Purpose:

1. Exercise
2. Moderate concealment and speed
3. Silent approach in dark
4. An attack position.

Position:

Holding your weapon, which may be anything from a Sten gun to a knife, in your right hand, kneel down on your *left* knee. Rest your right arm on your right knee which is *off* the ground. Crouch low.

How To Advance:

1. Left hand:

Cautiously feel along the ground in front of you with your left hand. Why? To find a silent spot in front of you. So don't put any weight on your left hand as you extend it. Separate your fingers (Fig. 5). When you have found a spot where leaves don't rustle, or boards don't squeak, then press your weight slowly onto your left hand. Then move your hand a couple of inches farther ahead (Fig. 6).

Fig. 5
Left Hand
Feel for a silent spot in front of you with your left hand.

Fig. 6
When you have found a silent spot, slowly press your weight onto your left hand.

2. Left knee:

Now lift up your left knee, and foot too, and quietly and gradually place your left knee down, immediately behind your left hand, on the silent spot (Figs. 7 and 8).

Fig. 7   Fig. 8
Slowly bring up your left knee behind your left hand.

A mistake commonly made is that the left foot is dragged noisily along the ground. Lift it up. Think of a tin can tied to a dog's tail, that's your left foot.

3. Left hand:

Now again reach out your left hand exploring the ground in front of you for a noiseless spot. When you find one rest your weight on it, pressing your hand down gradually (Figs. 9 and 10).

4. Right foot :

Now shift your weight over to the left side of your body and lift your right foot off the ground. Then gently swinging it around, feel lightly with your

HOW TO CRAWL

Fig. 9   Fig. 10

Reach out your left hand again, resting your weight on it when you find a silent spot.

right toe for a silent spot in front of you. When you find one, place your right foot down slowly, then put your weight on it (Fig. 11).

Fig. 11

Lean over slightly to your left, shifting your weight off your right foot. Lift up your right foot and swinging it forward, feel with your toe for a silent spot, then step your right foot down on it.

5. Left Knee:

Now lift up your left knee and slowly press it down behind your left hand (Fig. 12).

Fig. 12

After resting your weight on your right foot, lift up your left knee and place it behind your left hand.

6. Then repeat, Left, hand!
Left, knee!
Left, hand!
Right, foot!
Left, knee!

(These are the commands for instructors to give.)

One should keep as low as possible while doing this silent semi-crawl, keeping alert. This is a good out-of-doors exercise. It should be practiced blind-folded. Crawling fifty yards on clear land, then on wooded land, then with sound and vision spotters, then live ammunition overhead, should be practised. The crawl should be practised at first with precision commands, then without commands, until it can be done correctly, almost subconsciously.

HOW TO CRAWL

WHAT TO DO, IF

IF a hand-grenade explodes to your right :
Answer : Fall flatly to the ground, on your left side, perhaps firing in the direction from which the grenade came. Break the fall by striking the ground flatly, and simultaneously, with the under surface of the left forearm and palm, on an area from your elbow to your fingertips (Fig. 13). Later, a method of breaking falls without injury is fully described.

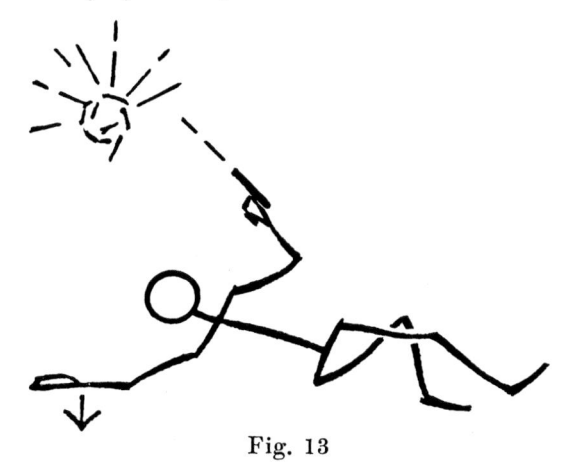

Fig. 13
Side Break-Fall From the Silent Semi-Crawl Position.

* * *

IF crawling forward in the Silent Semi-Crawl position, you suddenly meet one of the enemy crawling towards you, and you are unarmed, what can you do, fast and unexpected ?

Answer: 1. Break his jaw with a left knee blow (Fig. 14).
        2. Kick him under the chin with your left foot (Fig. 15).
        3. Kick him in the neck or head with your right foot (Fig. 16).

HOW ?

You are crouched down in the Semi-Crawl position, kneeling on your left knee. Your left foot is on the ground behind your left knee. Your right foot is on the ground and your right knee is *off* the ground directly above it.

8   ARWROLOGY

One of the following methods may be used.

1. Reach up both hands, clasping him behind the head or neck and tug his face down viciously into your left knee which is smashed up against his jaw (Fig. 14).

Fig. 14

Push his helmet back and his head down towards your left knee which you smash up to his jaw.

2. Lean back on your hands, and swing your left foot up from under you, kicking between his arms up under his chin (Fig. 15).

Fig. 15

Lean back on your hands, swinging up your left foot under his jaw.

HOW TO CRAWL

3. Lean over to your left. Swing your right foot around sideways kicking the left side of his head (Fig. 16).

Fig. 16
Lean over to your left swinging your right foot around against the right side of his head.

Fig. 17
Holding his arms at his sides, bring up your right knee into his crotch.

IF you are suddenly confronted by an enemy standing, facing you. What to do:

Take a short step forward with your left foot.

Spring up in front of him. Grasp both his arms firmly near the elbows, pressing them tightly to his body. At the same time bring your right knee up into his crotch or stomach with all the speed and force you can (Fig. 17).

What next?

Step Back Trip Throw

Holding his arms at his sides you may apply this throw which is described in detail farther on. Pull his left arm past your left side with your left hand and shove his left shoulder forward with your right hand. At the same time swing your right leg past the outside of his right leg and well behind both his legs. Twist him back over your right leg. Turn sharply to your left. Sag down on your left leg. A sharp pull with your left hand and a push with your right hand can speed up this throw.

Assault Trip Throw

OR—you may be able to do an Assault Trip Throw, described in detail farther on. With the left side of your body approaching his right side, bend down low, and plant your left leg behind his legs. Swing your left arm across the front of his chest and arms and scoop up his legs with your right arm by passing it behind him (Fig. 18).

Fig. 18
Assault Trip Throw

From his right side, lean down and put your left leg and right arm behind him, and your left arm across the front of his body.

Keep bent forward. Lever him over your left leg, turning to your left.

Lever him back off his feet.

After you have thrown him, what then?

Blows, kicks, Arwr locks!

If he resists, you pick up his right leg with your right arm and throw him over your left leg which you put tightly behind his left ankle.

MISCELLANEOUS POINTS
Stomach Throw

There is an old "stomach throw" which may be used here. With both hands, grab his upper arms or the front of his tunic, and place your left foot into his stomach or crotch (Fig. 19).

Roll over backwards. Pull him to you with your arms and kick him up high with your left foot, throwing him over your head. Actually you may use either your left or right foot depending on the circumstance (Figs. 19 and 20).

Fig. 19
Grab his arms. Put your left foot in his stomach. Fall backwards, kicking him over your head.

Fig. 20
Actually you may put either foot in his stomach. Here the right foot is used.

If you keep your grip on his clothing, a backward somersault will then land you on his chest.

12   ARWROLOGY

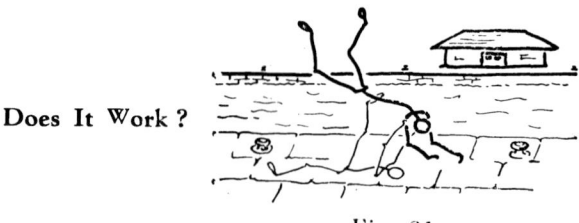

Does It Work ?

Fig. 21

It has. One day in the summer of 1942 a man tried to push Mr. J. B. into a canal. In the scuffle, Mr. J. B. grabbed his opponent near the shoulders and threw him over his head with the "stomach throw", then he applied an Arwr lock on his assailant's neck, with restraining results (Fig. 21).

Falling

From the Silent Semi-Crawl position, practice throwing yourself forward, breaking your short fall by landing on your forearms (Fig. 22). Sometimes it is harder to throw yourself to the ground than to throw an opponent there. There is often a certain reluctance about falling flat on your face. The exercises in Break Falls described farther should help to correct this fear.

Practice with rifles, learning to assume a firing position as soon as you have fallen.

Incidentally if you are running with a rifle and you suddenly wish to throw yourself to the ground, break your fall by grabbing the rifle near its centre with both hands and as you fall forward slam the rifle butt to the ground ahead of you, breaking the force of your fall.

Fig. 22

Practise falling forward onto your forearms from the Semi-Crawl position.

HOW TO CRAWL

Your Back

Remember that your back is always exposed from behind when you are crawling forward alone. Be cautious of an enemy stalking up behind you, or being in a tree above you. He may jump onto your back. Turn to your left if he does. Keep arms and knee moving, against him.

ADDITIONAL NOTES FROM INSTRUCTOR ON CHAPTER 1

Chapter 2

INTRODUCTION

WHY ?

CALISTHENICS for the armed forces should have at least two major objectives: First to prepare the soldier to overcome natural obstacles such as cliffs to climb, swamps to wade through, stretches of open country to run across, and miles to march. Second, to prepare the soldier to overcome the enemy in physical combat when the occasion of hand-to-hand fighting arises. From both aspects calisthenics are hardening exercises and should help to develop that last ounce of energy called stamina.

But calisthenics could contribute much more if they were more carefully selected and prepared for actual usefulness. And herein lies an importunate need. There is a psychological, and a prophylactic aspect, at presen' both in an inchoate state. These have not been sufficiently developed. However, some advances have been made with the introduction of Commando and Ranger training with live ammunition, endurance tests in the open and so on.

Psychologically speaking if an average unarmed man is taught the methods of overcoming armed opponents, and especially if he has been groomed in the technique of overcoming simultaneous attacks by "many" men, then he may be able to project and to sublimate this built up self-confidence and ability to cope imperturbably with problems of overwhelming odds into his actual fighting, whether it be one lonely British Mosquito or Spitfire, or one American Curtis SB2C-1 against four Ju-88 Stuka dive bombers, or one American medium M-3 tank against four of Hitler's heavy tanks, or one destroyer against four of the late Admiral Yamamoto's ships. He will consider himself as equipollent. Given the tools and this sense of high personal regard, our soldiers will unite them in quicker victory.

A series of *'one man against many'* calisthenics, wherein every movement is a specific one for offense or defence, wherein every movement may be used in actual combat, has a specific practical and psychological value.

Calisthenics could be more specialized, especially in the schools which will train instructors in the art of commando and guerilla fighting. Instead of generalized exercises with archaic knee bending and arm raising motions, directed at no specific future action on the battlefield, in the street, or in the concentration camp, there should be included a series of exercises which will serve some specific duty in actual combat, and help the soldier, on battlefields.

Let the arms above the head raising exercises be left for the Nazi. Let our men develop their muscles, neuro-muscular co-ordination and general health by having their calisthenics include such practical methods as falling flatly within a second, flatly forward, without injurying themselves, so that in bomb blasts they may be able to attain a safe prone position on the ground as quickly as humanly possible.

It has been estimated that fragmentation of an ordinary hundred pound bomb, exploding in an open street, is dangerous to anyone standing within two hundred feet. But a soldier caught in the street may survive by knowing how to take proper cover. Fragments are deflected upward from the crater, creating a fairly safe area on the ground beyond ten yards. So a soldier who knows how to fall flatly forward in an instantaneous manner would have a greater chance of survival than another who could not get down as quickly. Besides this, exercises in methods of breaking falls without injury would eliminate many accidents from falls which may disable a soldier just as effectively as a bullet would.

One has only to inspect the Out-Door records of any large hospital to appreciate the great number of injuries produced by slipping and falling incorrectly (Figs. 23, 24, 25, 26, 27, 28). Wrists, vertebrae, hips, ribs, ankles, fractured; head injuries and even dislocation of fingers, occur every year with appalling frequency.

In one large Canadian hospital I visited airmen laid up with broken arms, and soldiers hospitalized with broken legs, one case terminating by death, all partly because they did not know how to fall correctly.

18   ARWROLOGY

Anything Can Happen If You Do Not Know
How To Fall Without Injury

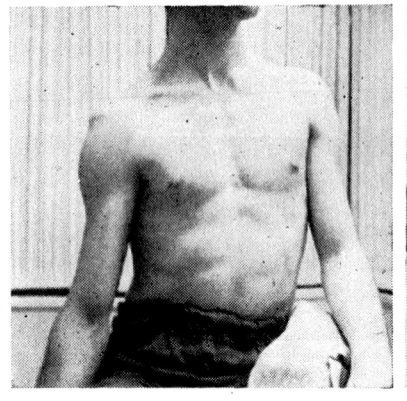

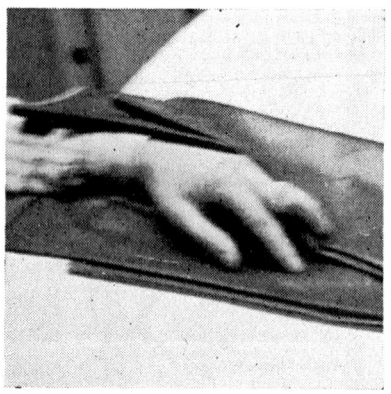

Fig. 23
A dislocated right shoulder.

Fig. 24
A dislocated finger.

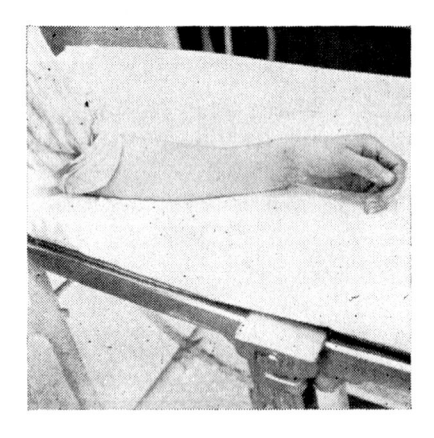

Fig. 25
A broken wrist.

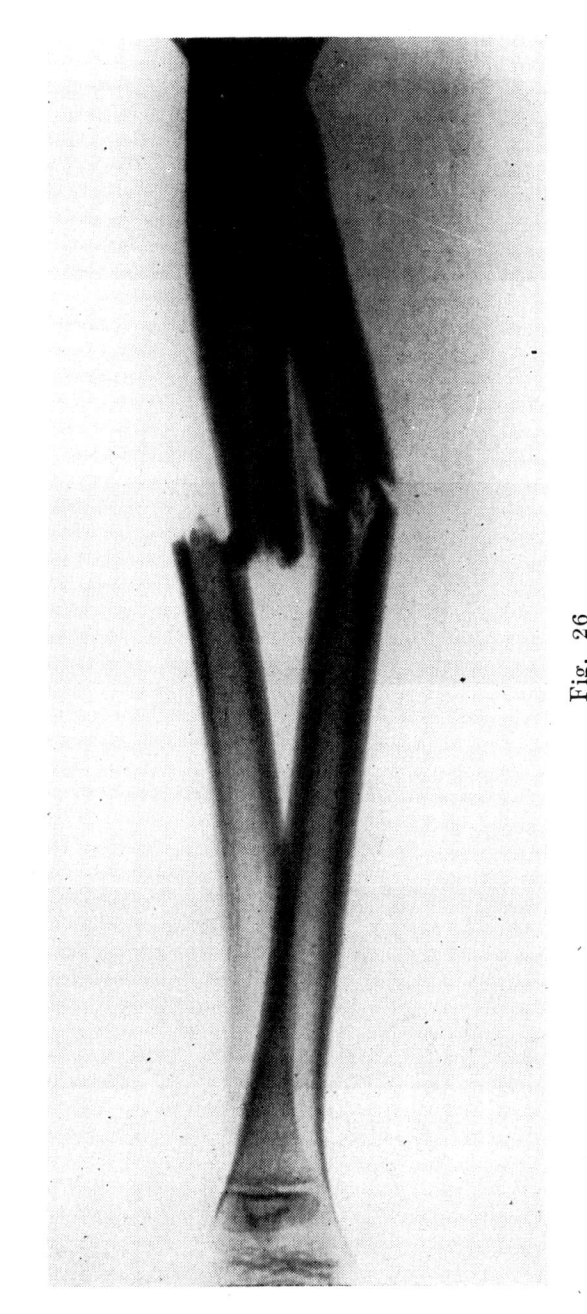

Fig. 26
X-Ray of a broken arm.

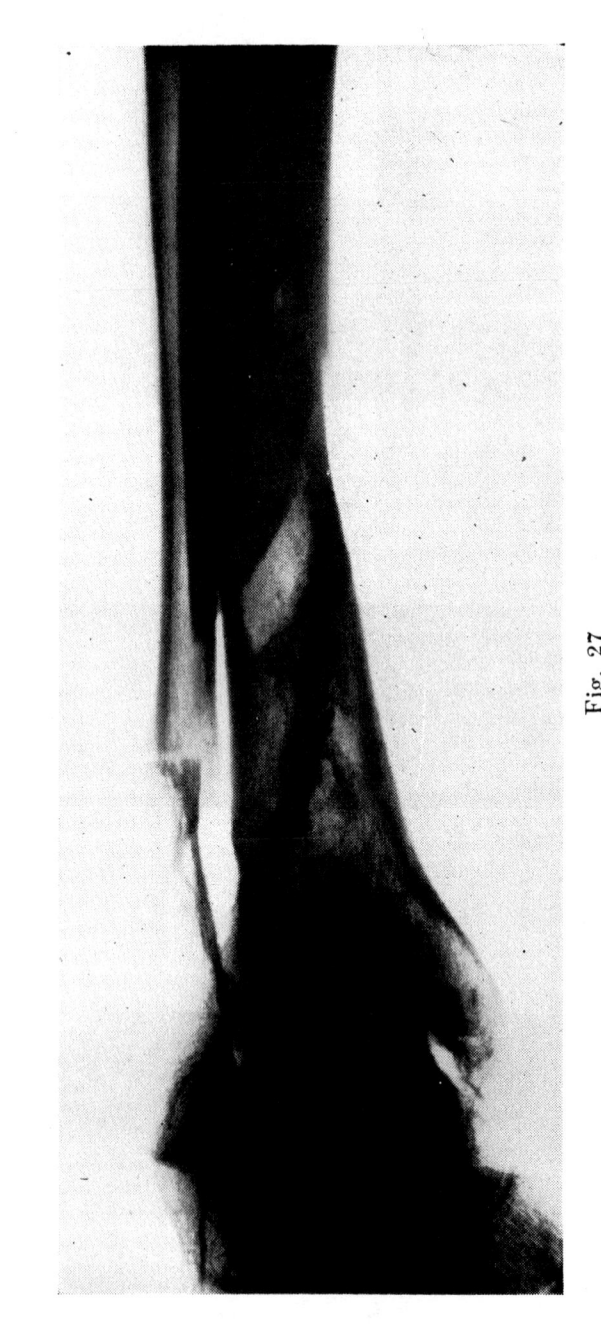

Fig. 27
X-Ray of a broken leg.

Fig. 28
X-Ray of a broken arm.

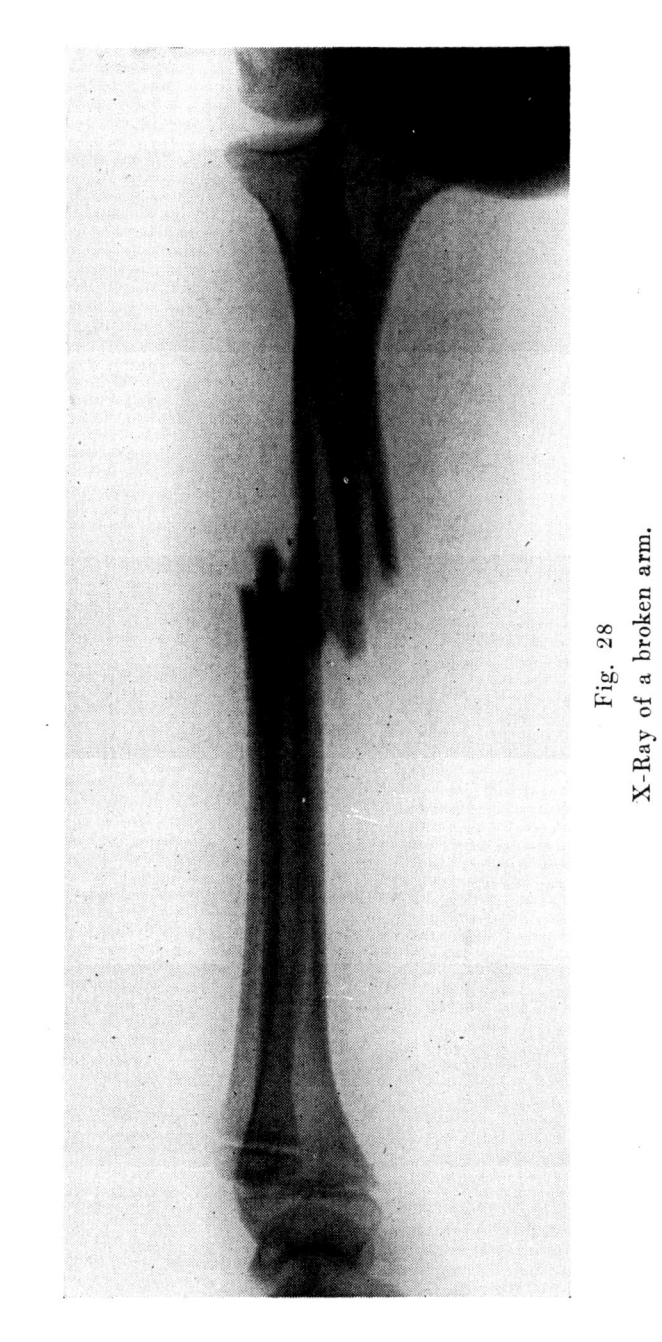

HOW?

From a preventative aspect there are two points worthy of mention.

1. How to fall without injury.

2. How to rise up from a sitting position without using the hands.

HOW TO FALL WITHOUT INJURY

One effective method of falling without injury is based on the theory that the larger the area of immediate contact, the less will be the force of impact at any one point of contact. So instead of falling on an outstretched hand, one of the most common mistakes, the ground should be struck with a larger area than just a hand or wrist. What will that be?

When falling, after being tripped or thrown, one should turn sideways and strike the ground flatly with an area, extending from the tip of the fingers to the elbow. This area including the palm and under surface of the forearm, should strike the ground simultaneously. Thumb and fingers should be kept tightly together and out straight.

One must gradually develop a conditioned-reflex to be able to do this. That is where calisthenics come in.

One exercise suggested is that the soldier should assume a *Crossed Legs Position* by sitting down with his left leg crossed in front of his right, like the old sitting position of tailors (Fig. 29).

From this position he should fall over to his right side, then push himself over to fall to his left side, then to his right again, and so on.

When he falls over to one side he should try to strike the ground *as hard as he can,* flatly with his (1) palm, (2) wrist and (3) the under surface of his forearm to his elbow. All these areas should strike the ground simultaneously in one motion.

The fingers are to be held tightly together, and out straight. This is the first stage of the exercise (Fig. 29).

The Crossed Legs Position

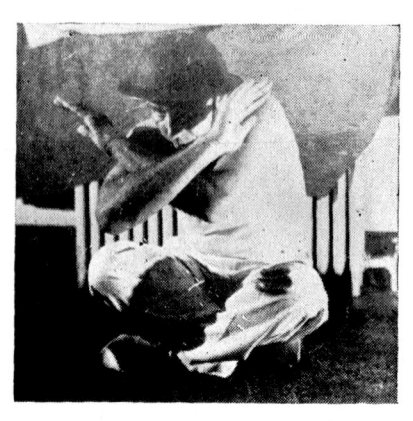

Fig. 29

Sit down with left leg crossed in front of the right. You can cross your right hand in front of your left. This is a defence position against frontal attack when you are down. You can guard your body and face with your arms and defend yourself against kicks with your feet.

This Crossed Legs Position is the first position from which to practice the *Break Fall*, the *Straight Rise Up* and the *Spin To The Feet* calisthenics.

* * *

Next he should rise to a little higher position. He should kneel forward on his knees, with knees together and feet out straight behind, like praying (Fig. 30).

From here he should practice falling to his right (Fig. 31), and then to his left, breaking his fall with his right, then left arm, in the manner described. Then he should fall face forward, breaking the fall with both arms out in front, striking the ground flatly from finger tips to elbows.

(One thing to do amuse yourself during a Black-Out is to practice Arwrology. Many of the photographs were taken under just such a circumstance.)

HOW TO FALL WITHOUT INJURY

Fig. 30
Get up on your knees.

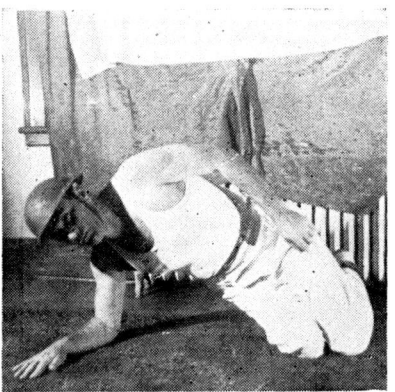

Fig. 31
Fall to your right, breaking the fall by striking the ground flatly with the under surface of your right forearm and open palm.

(Then push yourself over to your left and fall on your left arm in the same manner. Practise falling side to side from this position, then practise falling face forward breaking the fall with both arms out in front, striking the ground flatly from elbows to finger tips.)

* * *

The next position is to get up on the toes and crouch down on the heels, with bent knees off the ground, like the position taken after jumping down off a fence (Fig. 32). From here the practise of falling to the right and then to the left and then forward should be carried out as above.

* * *

Next stand upright and fall face forward, breaking the fall with both arms (Figs. 33 and 34).

26 ARWROLOGY

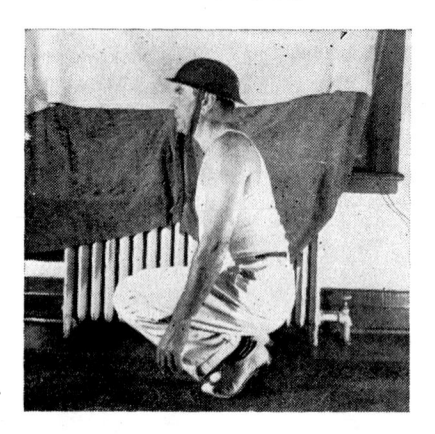

Fig. 32

Next sit up, balancing on your toes. Then practice falling to the right and then to the left.

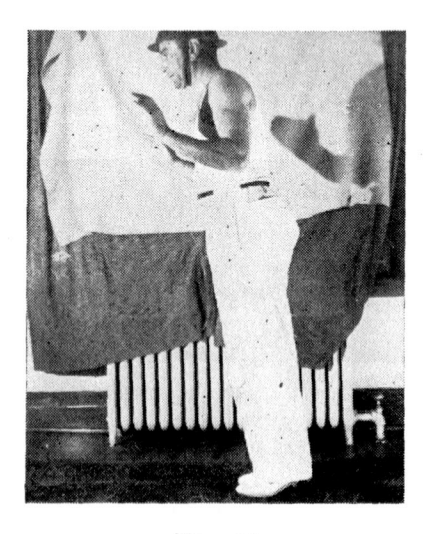

Fig. 33

Now stand upright. Lean **forward**.

HOW TO FALL WITHOUT INJURY

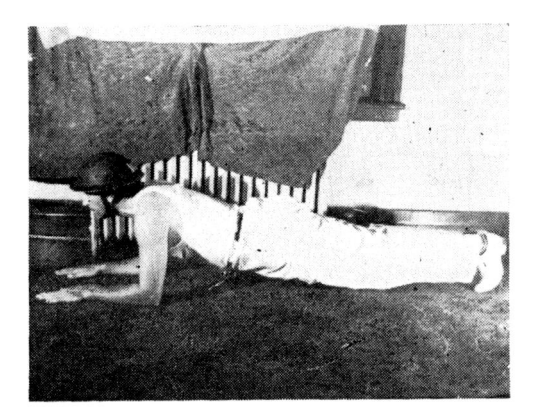

Fig. 34

Fall face forward, breaking the fall by striking the ground flatly and simultaneously with both palms and forearms. Keep your knees off the ground.

DOES IT WORK? It has. In 1937 in Ethopia, Dr. P. Roberts asserts that a man working with the Red Cross was caught in an open market-place during a bombing raid, and by falling face forward when a bomb exploded about fifty feet away he escaped injury, although being showered with dirt and debris (Fig. 35).

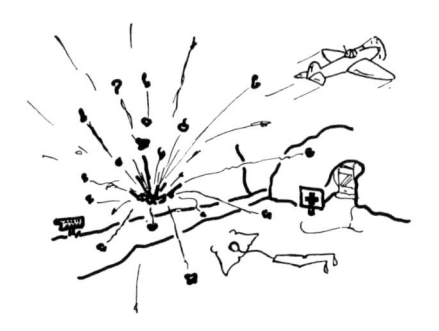

Fig. 35

HOW TO RISE UP FROM A SITTING POSITION WITHOUT USING THE HANDS

There are two other exercises which may be of some practical, psychological and therapeutic value. Therapeutically they may help to prevent flat feet and weak ankles.

1. The "Straight Rise Up" Exercise.

Assume the *Crossed Legs Position,* sitting down with left leg crossed in front of the right. Your right arm is crossed in front of your left (Fig. 29), or you may cross your left arm in front of your right (Fig. 38), depending on which method gives you easier balance. The purpose is to rise straight up to your feet without aid of hands. As you rise up shoot your arms up in front of you, palms forward, or you may hold a rifle with bayonet in your hands, thrusting it forward as you rise up vertically.

Some men will find great difficulty in trying to rise without using their hands, due to lack of balance and practice. At first, you may put your hands on the ground on either side giving yourself a push (Fig. 36). Then, after practice, try to rise without using your hands. Try shooting up your arms as you rise (Fig. 37). Keep your feet in the same position.

A good method of learning this exercise is to place chairs, one on either side of you, and sit on the floor between them. Put a hand on each chair, and, with the assistance of your arms, rise up straight from the *Crossed Legs Position.* When you have acquired sufficient ability do not use the chairs.

HOW TO RISE UP

Fig. 36

At first it may be necessary to push yourself up with the aid of your hands.

Fig. 37

From the *Crossed Legs Position* (Fig. 29), rise straight up without any assistance from your hands and not moving your feet, but pushing with the outside edges of your feet. Thrust up with your hands, palms forward, as though you were reaching up at someone's throat. Later hold a rifle with bayonet and thrust up as you rise. This exercise can develop balance, and muscles of the feet, legs and abdomen. It can strengthen the feet and ankles particularly.

2. The "Spin To The Feet" Exercise.

This is another exercise which enables a man to rise to his feet without use of his arms. It is very fast.

Instructions:

1. Sit down in the *Crossed Legs Position,* with left leg crossed in front of your right. Tuck your feet well in. Cross your left arm up in front of your right. Crouch forward slightly (Fig. 38).

> (The next movements are to be carried out rhythmically, in one motion. You are to spin to your right rising up at the same time with the suddenness of a whirlwind. The force and speed of the spin give power to an edge-hand blow which you may deliver with the little finger edge of your right hand at an opponent who faces you.)

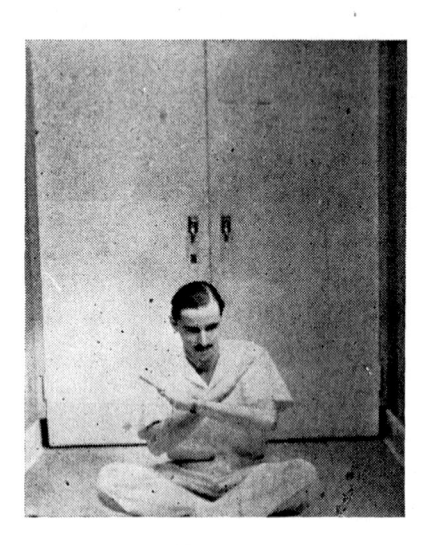

Fig. 38

Sit down in the *Crossed Legs Position.* Left leg is crossed in front of the right. Here left arm is crossed in front of the right. Tuck your feet in close to you.

HOW TO RISE UP

2. To start the spin to your feet, lean forward so only the outside edges of your feet are on the ground. Stretch out your arms a little for balance. Grip the floor with the little toe edge of your feet (Fig. 39).

3. Rise up from here, using your leg muscles. Keep your arms crossed in the defence position (Fig. 40).

Fig. 39　　　　　　　　　　Fig. 40

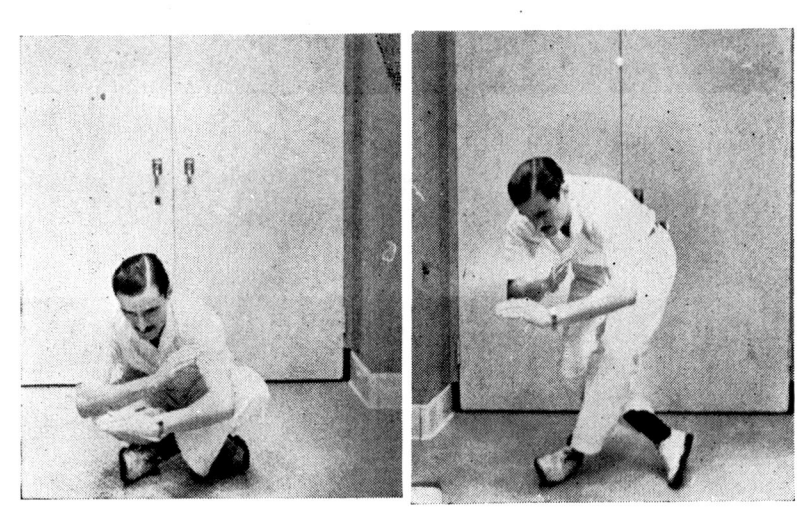

Fig. 39

Lean forward, balancing on the outside edges of your feet, with the rest of your body *off* the ground. Put your arms out a little in front to maintain balance. You are beginning to rise up now.

Fig. 40

Rise up higher by straightening your legs. Start to turn to your right. Note that all your weight is balanced on the little toe edge of your feet.

32   ARWROLOGY

4. As you rise, turn right (Fig. 41).

5. As you turn keep your right shoulder hunched up a little, tucking your chin behind it (Fig. 42).

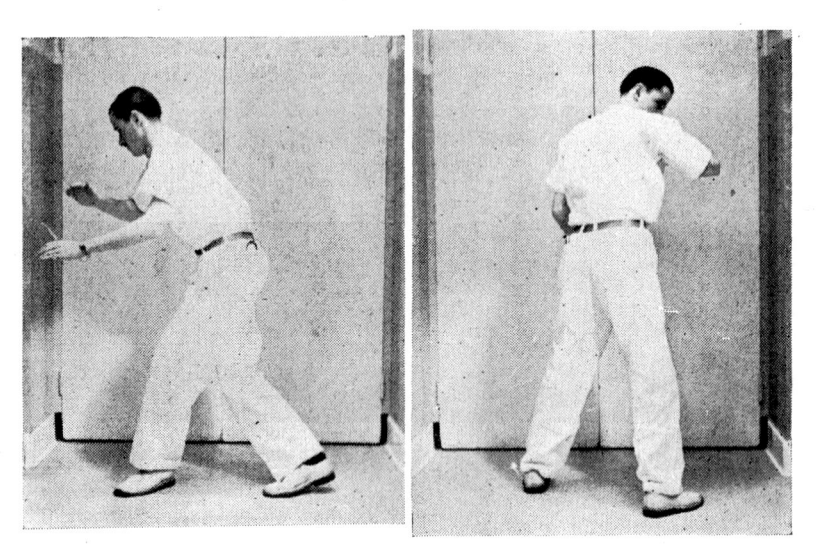

Fig. 41
Straighten up higher, turning more to your right. Hold your right hand out stiffly like a board.

Fig. 42
Turn right around. This is all one motion!

6. You should always come up from this spin prepared to fight. So cock your right forearm and hand out stiffly as you turn around, prepared to give an edge-hand blow (Fig. 43).

7. Swing the blow up, like a back-hand stroke in tennis, at the neck of any opponent facing you. Use the force of your right spin (Fig. 44).

HOW TO RISE UP

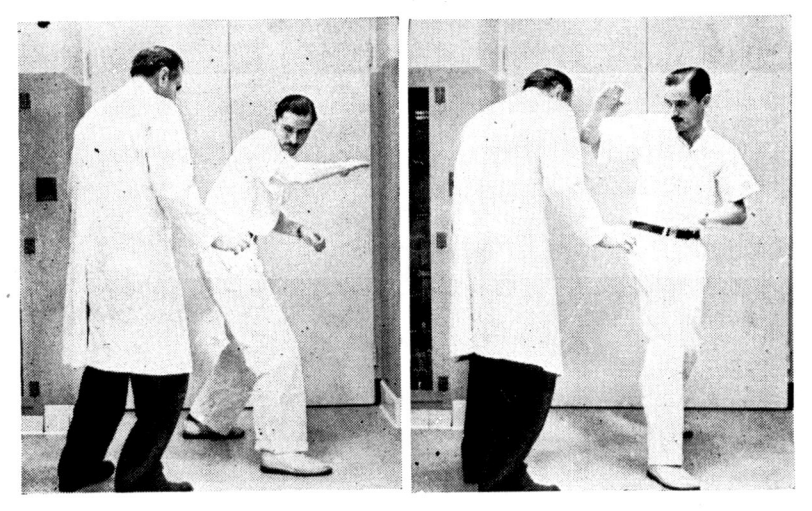

Fig. 43   Fig. 44

Fig. 43
Suppose there is an opponent in front of you. He may have knocked you down and you have just spun up to your feet. Your right arm is bent like an Australian boomerang, horizontal with the floor at this stage.

Fig. 44
Complete the spin around aiming the little finger edge of your stiffened right hand at the right side of his neck. (The Carotid Sinus blow.)

8. Try to strike the region of the Carotid Sinus on the side of his neck, generally on a level with the top of his "Adam's Apple", and with your left hand keep his right arm down from obstructing your blow.

Your left hand plays interference. Make your right hand slide along the edge of his neck in a follow-through motion, striking steadily around to your right (Fig. 45).

Then follow up with knee blows, ultimately securing an Arwr Lock.

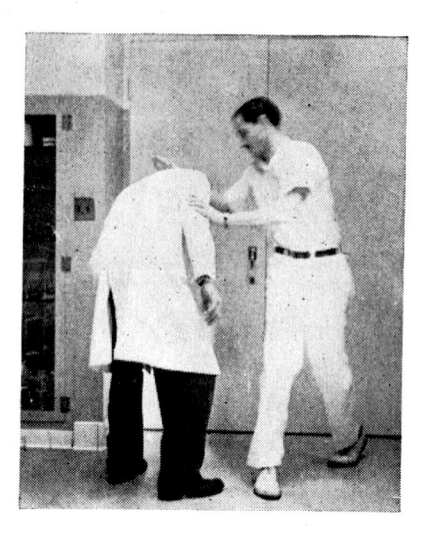

Fig. 45

With your left hand keep his right arm down and suddenly deliver the edge-hand blow with your right hand.

Situations

In the study of Arwrology, various positions are studied from which an opponent may attack you or in which you may be when he attacks. This is directed at giving you greater reaction speed than your opponent. It robs him of the element of surprise and in turn often surprises him.

Briefly applying this *'Situation Study'* to spinning up to your feet, we may assume that you have been thrown flat on your back, or flat on your face. How can you get up to your feet in the quickest manner?

Preparative Exercises :

1.—*From Flat On Your Back.*

1. Lie flat on your back with arms and legs outstretched.

HOW TO RISE UP

2. Still lying on your back, bend up your legs with left ankle crossed over the front of the right, and at the same time cross your left wrist over the front of your right wrist. Hunch up tightly in this defence position on your back.
3. Reach your left hand down and grasp your left ankle.
4. Pull yourself up to the *Crossed Legs Position* (Fig. 38), with left ankle crossed in *front* of your right.
5. From there rise *straight* up, or *spin* to your right, up to your feet, as already described.

If you wish to spin to your left, reach your right hand down and grasp your right ankle which you cross *in front* of your left ankle (Fig. 29).

Practise this exercise at first in individual steps. Then make it all one movement, developing grace and rhythm. Motions that are graceful and rhythmical can generally become very fast.

2.—*From Flat On Your Face.*

1. Lie down flat on your face with arms and legs outstretched.
2. Roll over onto your left side. With your left hand push yourself up into the *Crossed Legs Position,* with left leg crossed in front of the right (Fig. 46). Then spin up to your feet turning around to your right.

Fig. 46

Lying flat on your face roll to your right, pushing yourself up with your left hand into the *Crossed Legs Position.*

K. B. S.

Know Both Sides. After mastering the exercises as described here, if you still have interest and ambition, try the methods reversing right for left, and left for right. Be an ambidexterous fighter. Have no weak side.

Don't Be A Specialist

If you know any boxing or wrestling or other type of fighting, do not neglect that knowledge. The methods described here are to assist you in fighting, not to replace everything you know about fighting. Utilize every resource.

Summary

A method of falling without injury and of rising without use of hands is mentioned which may be used in military calisthenics. The latter exercise may have a prophylactic and therapeutic effect in flat feet and allied conditions.

A more practical type of calisthenics is urged with more importance being given to the psychological phase.

ADDITIONAL NOTES FROM INSTRUCTOR ON CHAPTER 2.

Chapter 3

KNEE-BLOW PSYCHO-PHYSICAL CALISTHENICS

FOR ONE TO A THOUSAND MEN

Directions:

STAND at attention and stretch your arms out straight in front of you (Fig. 47).

Suddenly bring up your left knee as high as you can towards your left hand (Fig. 48).

Fig. 47
Attention! Arms, Out!

Fig. 48
Left, Knee!

40   ARWROLOGY

Then step forward and down with your left foot (Fig. 49).

Then bring up your right knee high as you can and with all the force you can muster. Bring it up towards your right hand (Fig. 50).

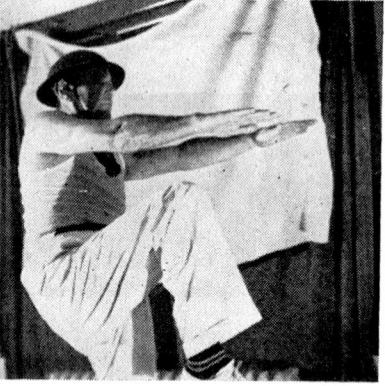

Fig. 49
Step!

Fig. 50
Right, Knee!

Then step forward with your right leg. Then left knee blow, left step forward, right knee blow, right step forward, left knee blow and so on.

Practise this marching various distances, for example fifty paces forward and then back. If you think this is sissy stuff, wait until you get those pains and that stiffness in the back of your tired legs next day. To prevent this, exercise a little the first day and gradually increase the amount.

Variation:

Strike Your Palms

Practice giving actual blows with your knees to your outstretched palms. Put force into the blows.

KNEE-BLOW PSYCHO-PHYSICAL CALISTHENICS 41

Psychological Aspect

Every time you strike your knees up, *think* of giving mighty knee blows up at your enemy's stomach or crotch. And in actual fighting, keep your knees driving into your opponent at every opportunity.

Don't forget that you are training to become an "Arwr", an All-Out Hand-To-Hand Fighter. Some men like to growl out the word "Arwr" like a war-cry when they strike their hands with their knees in the exercise. So if you feel like it, as you give the knee blows let out a good roar as though you were the Lion itself, and roll the R's like good Scots, "ArROORRR!"

A thousand Commandos or Rangers doing knee-blow psychophysical calisthenics, with a growl from a thousand throats breaking the air with every upward blow of the knees would engender remarkable enthusiasm.

Variation

Strike Your Palm With Each Knee Blow

Fig. 51 — Right, Knee!

Fig. 52 — Left, Knee!

ADDITIONAL NOTES FROM INSTRUCTOR ON CHAPTER 3

Chapter 4

UNARMED "BLOW POWER"

Hit him with everything you've got.

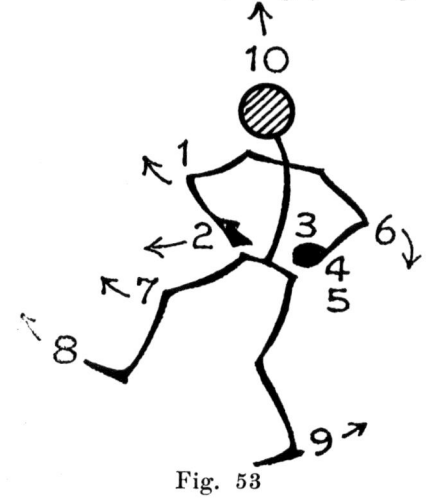

Fig. 53

1. Back of your elbow
2. Little finger edge of your out-stretched hand
3. Your fist, or
4. Your stiff finger tips, or
5. The heel of your palm
6. Front of your elbow
7. Your knee
8. Your toe
9. Back of your heel
10. Your head.

1. "THE BACK OF YOUR ELBOW". (Fig. 53 No. 1, Fig. 58, Fig. 61, Fig. 63 Nos. 2 and 6).

WHAT is *Unarmed Blow Power?* With unarmed blow power, you are expected to do everything except kick your opponent with both feet at the same time. (You can do that too if you are lying on the ground or if you can hang onto something to support your weight.) Literally unarmed blow power is hitting an opponent with everything you've got. What does that include? (Fig. 53).

Where?

(a) (Carotid Sinus)

Either side of his neck, at about the level of the top of his Adam's Apple. The carotid artery in the neck divides about there into two branches. Where it divides, there is a small structure including the Carotid Body and Sinus. A blow over this spot has a tendency to knock a man out quickly.

(b) *The temple,* about an inch above and in front of the top of his ears. Here you have a chance of injuring the middle meningeal artery if you fracture his skull. The artery is inside the skull and if it is torn, death may result.

(c) *Jaw.* Anyone who has done any boxing knows that a hard blow to the side of the jaw can occasionally knock a man out.

(d) *Ribs.* Under his arms. Hit ribs with horizontal blows, along the line of the ribs.

(e) *'Stomach'*. Hit him in his abdomen in the midline just below his lower ribs.

(f) *Crotch*. Between his legs. A vertical upward blow works best here. If this bends him forward, force his head down and give it a knee blow, or immediately come up with the back of your elbow, this time under his chin. Follow up with edge-hand blows to the side of his neck.

(g) *His upper legs.* (1) The *outside* of his leg half way up between his knee and hip. This works best if his weight is on the leg struck. When the tensor fascia lata muscle here is struck forcefully, a painful paralyzing effect in the leg is often produced. A knee blow works especially well here.

Does It Work? An Actual Case.

About a year ago I attended a man in a hospital who had had his right leg struck in this region. The pain and lameness which resulted suggested a fracture of the upper bone in the leg, but X-Ray examination ruled this out.

His leg was paralyzed for over three days.

(2) The *inside* of his leg about a third of the way down from his crotch to his knee. Here we strike against the region of the femoral artery and the saphenous nerve. This can be one of the most sensitive spots in the body. The Assault Trip Throw, described later, is often a good follow-up from this blow.

Both these blows should contact *against the bone* of your opponent's upper leg.

2. "THE LITTLE FINGER EDGE OF YOUR HAND". (Fig. 54, also Fig. 53 No. 2, Figs. 55, 59, 62, 63 Nos. 3 and 7.)

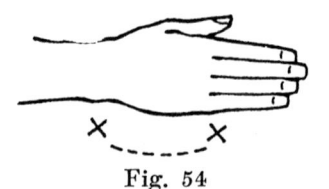

Fig. 54

STRIKE with the little finger edge of your out-stretched hand from the base of your little finger to your wrist. Keep your fingers tightly pressed together, and keep your thumb in close too. Your palm nearly always faces *down*.

This is probably the most deadly natural weapon that an unarmed man possesses if he knows how to use it.

Fig. 55

Make the edge-hand blow snappy. Cut it. Don't just push.

How is it used? Look at your right hand. Straighten out your fingers and thumb. Press them close together. Straighten out your hand, wrist and forearm so they form a straight line. You strike with the little finger edge of that hand, from the base of your little finger to about an inch up from your wrist. You deliver the blows with your palm facing down.

Feel the little finger edge of your hand. It is probably soft. It must be hard. How are you going to harden it? Straighten out your hand and with the little finger edge strike repeatedly against any hard surface.

At first these blows may be delivered as light, chopping strokes. As the hand becomes used to the exercise and acquires resistance, more severe blows may be given, until finally a powerful blow with the full, back-hand sweep of the arm is possible. Practice the blows against tables, walls, sand-bags, poles, doors, anything.

EDGE-HAND BLOW EXERCISE

Horizontal Blows.

1.—Face a wall. Keeping your feet still, turn left, bringing your right hand over your left shoulder. Swing to your right, striking the wall at the level of your own neck with the little finger edge of your right hand. Put force into it. Then twist further to your right, bringing your left hand over your right shoulder, *keeping your feet still.* Swing to your left, striking the wall at the level of your neck with the little finger edge of your left hand. Repeat these actions over and over.

* * *

2.—Now stand with your left side against the wall. Put your left shoulder against it. You are standing at a right angle to the wall. Do not move your feet. Turn left twisting about as far as you can, bringing your right hand over your left shoulder. Unwind and strike the wall with the little finger edge of your stiffened out right hand. Give a hard blow. You are using your waist muscles to advantage.

Keeping your feet in the same position, turn right and bring your left hand over your right shoulder. Deliver a back edge-hand blow against the wall with your left hand.

* * *

3.—Next stand with your right side against the wall, and repeat the right and left hand blows as above. Rub alcohol on the edge of your hands if they get tender.

* * *

4.—Next stand with your back to the wall, and keeping your feet motionless, practice striking the wall with your right and left hand, twisting at the waist with each blow.

These blows have been *horizontal*. Next come the *vertical* edge-hand blows.

Vertical Blows

Facing a wall, turn to your left, just from the waist, keeping your feet still. Give an upward blow against the wall with the little finger edge of your right hand. Then turn left and give an upward blow with your left hand. Repeat.

* * *

By now you will have an idea of the Edge-Hand blows. *Where* are you going to hit your opponent with the Edge-Hand blows?

UNARMED "BLOW POWER"

Remember these points

(a) Either side of his neck (Carotid Sinus).

(b) The back of his neck, at a point just above the hair line. Why here? Respiratory centres may be affected by a blow in this region.

(c) Just above and below his nose.

(d) Along one of his ribs. Here give a *horizontal* blow, directly under his arms or a little behind his arms. A blow in the region of the kidneys has a shocking effect. This blow is also effective over his heart.

(e) Up into his crotch. Give a *vertical* blow here.

(f) 'Stomach'. Just under his ribs in the front of his body in the mid-line.

(g) Forearm. Against the top of his forearm at the junction of the upper third and lower two thirds (Brachio-radialis muscle and posterior interroseous nerve).

Do the Edge-Hand Blows work? They have!

Fig. 56

An Actual Case

In 1941, Mr. J. J. who is a member of the Society of Arwrologists was walking home one night past a field when he was attacked from behind by four men. One man pulled him around and stuck him a glancing blow on the side of his face.

Mr. J. J. ducked down and swung around delivering a left edge-hand blow against the side of the man's neck (Carotid Sinus).

What happened? The man's arms dropped to his sides and he fell forward, flat on his face. The knock-out was absolutely instantaneous.

Two of the men looked with amazement for a moment, then ran. And when Mr. J. J. turned towards the remaining opponent, he ran too.

With a wave of his hand and a "Good night, gentlemen," Mr. J. J. continued on his way home, smiling confidently.

* * *

Another Actual Case

One February evening in 1943, another member of the Society of Arwrologists reports that he was attacked by a man in a cigar store. A back edge-hand blow was delivered under the man's ear. The man fell to the floor, sick to his stomach, hors de combat.

* * *

3. "YOUR FIST". Strike face, side of jaw, stomach, under the arms, over the heart.

4. "STIFF FINGER TIPS". (a) Jab these into his eyes. Jab with your palm facing down, and slide your fingers into his eye along the cheek bone under his eye. Keep your fingers tightly together. Follow up by twisting his head around and getting a Posterior Arwr lock. (Described farther on).

(b) Jab up under his jaw. (Submaxillary glands and digastric muscles. This can produce a painful 'lockjaw' condition.)

(c) Jab under his ear, behind the angle of his jaw. (Parotid gland. Forceful pressure here with a finger tip is a good trick to revive quickly a comrade who has been knocked out.)

5. "BASE OF PALM". A sharp upward blow or push with the heel of your palm against the side of his jaw, the back of his head, or over his heart or stomach often upsets an opponent long enough for you to follow up with something more effective.

Example : Standing at the left of your opponent, strike the left side of his jaw with the heel of your open left hand. Then jump behind him and with your open right hand push the back of his head to your left, while your left hand pushes his jaw to your right. Then slide your arms into a Posterior Arwr lock, with *left* forearm across the front of his neck. (Arwr locks are described farther on).

6. "FRONT OF ELBOW". Sometimes you can swing the front of your elbow against a man's jaw.

7. "KNEE". A high knee blow to the crotch or outside of thigh is effective when a man is standing. When your opponent is down, a knee blow to the temple, spine or ribs is often effective.

8. "KICKS WITH YOUR TOE". When your opponent is standing, remember to kick against his shin, especially immediately after giving a knee blow to his crotch. If you feel acrobatic, or have had experience in foot-ball or soccer, a kick to the crotch or under the chin may be attempted.

When your opponent is down, you may kick him in the temple, side or back of his neck, crotch, ribs or spine.

9. "KICKS WITH YOUR HEEL". Very important. Not emphasized enough. When your opponent is standing kick back at him against the shin and the back of his leg at whatever opportunity you have.

When your opponent is down remember the above mentioned locations.

Kicks with the *outside edge of your foot* are effective. Side kicks are generally more reliable than straight forward kicks. (See "Kicking Practice" farther on.)

10. "HELMET". If your have a helmet on, use the top for butting and the front rim for cutting down blows into your opponent's face. If your enemy has a strap under his chin holding his helmet on his head, from behind him you can jerk the helmet back off his head so the strap catches him across the front of his neck.

(1) *BACK-ELBOW AND EDGE-HAND BLOW CALISTHENICS WITH A PARTNER.* (Figs. 57, 58, 59, 60, 61, 62).

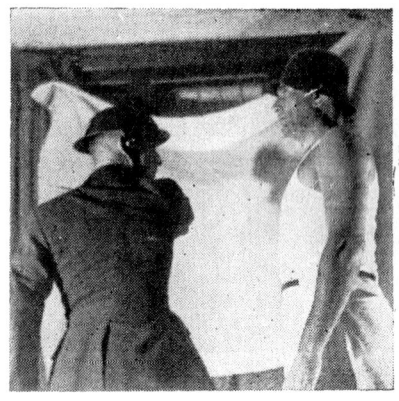

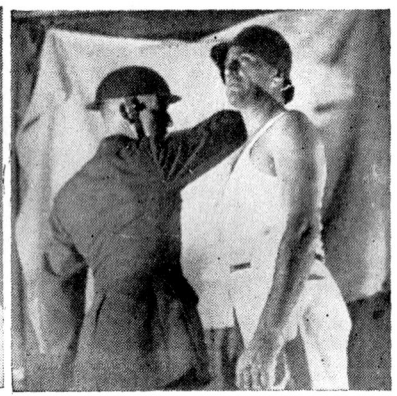

Fig. 57

Fig. 58

Fig. 57—Face your partner, who substitutes for one of the enemy. Stiffen out your right hand like a board, with your fingers held firmly together, and turning to your left swing your right hand over your left shoulder.

Fig. 58—Swing the back of your right elbow against the right side of his neck (Carotid Sinus).

UNARMED "BLOW POWER"

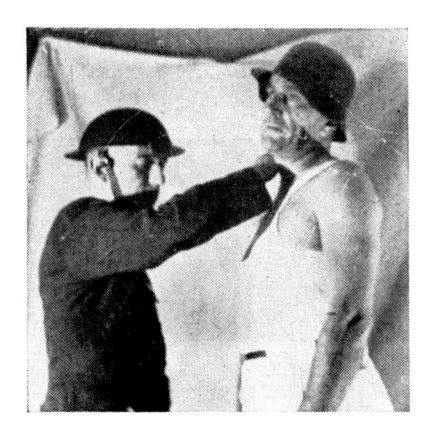

Fig. 59

Follow this up with a blow against the same spot with the little finger edge of your right hand.

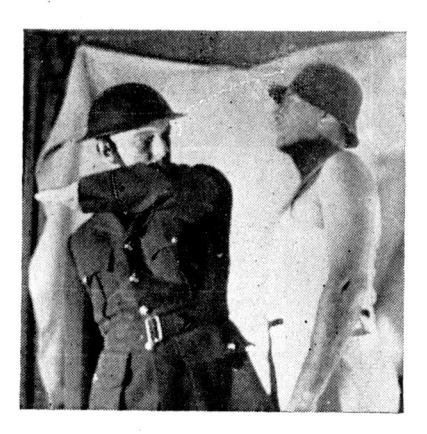

Fig. 60

Then swing around to your right bringing your left hand over your right shoulder, aiming the back of your left elbow at the left side of his neck.

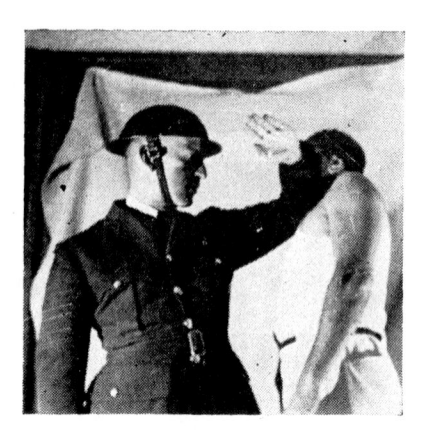

Fig. 61

Swing the back of your left elbow against the left side of his neck (Carotid Sinus).

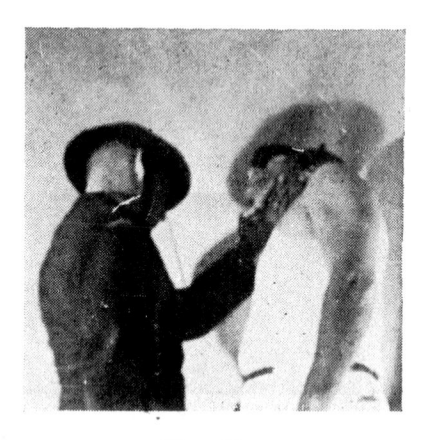

Fig. 62

Follow up with a cutting blow against the same spot with the little finger edge of your left hand.

Repeat this procedure over and over, starting at Fig. 57. Count the blows out loud. Gradually speed up the blows after accuracy has been attained. Naturally do not deliver hard blows here.

(2) 'BLOW POWER' PRACTICE WITH A SAND-BAG. (Fig. 63).

Fig. 63

Face a sand-bag, getting right up close to it.
(A wall or post may be substituted for a sand-bag.)

1. Bring your right hand across your left shoulder.
2. Strike the sand-bag with the back of your right elbow.
3. Next with the little finger edge of your stiffened out right hand, fingers held tightly together.
4. Next with your left fist. (Like the "straight left" blow in boxing). At the same time bring up your left knee for a high knee blow.
5. Next with the front of your left elbow.
6. Next with the back of your left elbow.
7. Next with the edge of your left hand.
8. Next with your right fist, also giving a right knee blow.
9. Next with the front of your right elbow.

Keep pressing forward all the time.
Repeat the cycle of blows over and over until you have attained your maximum speed. Deliver hard blows.

Do The Blows Work? They Have!

AN ACTUAL CASE : Late in the night of March 20th, 1943, in Montreal, Mr. J., who is an instructor in the Society of Arwrologists was attacked from behind by four men.

In his report to the Society he states that he was waiting for a bus which he saw coming towards him far in the distance, when someone grabbed him around the waist from behind.

He whirled around to his right, delivering a blow to his assailant's chest with the back of his right elbow. Then he gave another right elbow blow to the man's neck, followed by a right edge-hand blow to the neck again.

The second opponent who was behind him was disposed of by a similar right edge-hand blow to the neck (Carotid Sinus).

The third man rushed in and was twisted to the ground by a simple "Head Twist". (See Part V, Chapter 4).

The fourth man was standing back in the shadows and Mr. J. was not sure if he was part of the group attacking him or not, so he grabbed him anyway and threw him face forward by a throw similar to the one described in Part III, Chapter 3.

Mr. J. concluded his report by saying he didn't miss the bus!

SOME GENERAL POINTS

The trick is to be able to deliver these blows in sequence and as rapidly as possible. Sometimes you can give two or three together. If you do not hit your opponent with the first blow, you will probably hit him with the next or the next, if they come fast enough. Keep after him.

What is the purpose of the blows?

1.—To knock out your opponent.
2.—To lessen resistance so that a lock may be used to render him unconscious or break his neck.
3.—To get him into position for a throw which may be followed with a fatal lock or kick.

Remember one blow must follow the other. Keep your opponent on the defensive.

When practising the blows against a *partner*, do not hit too hard. It is important to learn the location for the blows. When you want to develop speed and force, strike against a wall, door, post or sand-bag.

At first have your partner stand with his arms down, in a passive manner, offering no defence, no resistance. When you know how to deliver the blows, then practise them having your opponent trying to guard against them. It is harder now. Give "soft" blows. Just see if you can touch the spots you aim at. Then have him not only defend himself against the blows, but also try to hit you. Naturally the blows are not to be delivered with force. There is all the difference in the world between trying to hit a man's neck when his arms are down and when his arms are up, in action. Therefore try to pull your opponent's arms away with one hand and hit him with the other.

Forward Crouch

When fighting, keep your body flexed, bent low and forward —a loose crouch. It gives more protection, better balance and springing power. The lower you crouch to the floor with your feet well separated, the harder it is for anyone to push you off balance. Resting your elbows on your knees helps to give you a firm balance.

"Crouch Walk" Exercise

A valuable exercise to develop springing posture and firm stance is to crouch down, then resting your elbows or forearms on your knees, walk about, swinging your left shoulder forward when your left foot advances and your right shoulder forward when your right foot advances. Maintain a firm balance. This is often a good position from which to attack.

"Jumping Attack" Exercise

Sometimes it is advantageous to spring up at your opponent. Practise against a long narrow sand-bag, hung up so it will support your weight. Creep up to it. Then jump up high, getting a scissors hold about it with your legs and clamping a Posterior Arwr lock (described farther on) on it with your arms. Practise leaping up high.

Your Neck

A strong neck is a valuable asset in fighting.

An exercise to strengthen the neck: The mental picture to imagine is that someone is going to grab you suddenly about the neck.

Tighten your neck muscles firmly. Shorten your neck by pulling your chin in and hunching up your shoulders. Try to make your ears touch your shoulders.

Then relax your neck and tighten it again, over and over.

If you exercise before a mirror, you may see the platysma muscle in the neck pulling up the skin of your upper chest, as the muscle gets more developed.

For Marching Soldiers

This is an exercise which may be practised by soldiers while they are marching. In this case the shoulders should be back, well braced.

The command is "Shorten, Neck!" Then after a period of a few minutes, the command "Relax, Neck!" may be given.

Weak Spot. When fighting, if you tighten your neck muscles, bend your waist to protect it from blows as your abdominal muscles may relax. (Reciprocal innervation.)

Abdominal Muscles

In fierce hand-to-hand fighting always remember to twist and turn even if you forget everything else. Twist away from facing your opponent and turn quickly towards him delivering back-elbow and edge-hand blows. Turn to one side and then to the other or turn right around coming back with powerful edge-hand blows. Use your abdominal muscles to put power into your short blows. Keep your body flexed, bent tightly.

When rolling on the ground, huddle up. Bend your arms. Bend up your legs. Bend your chin on your chest. Then kick out. Strike out. Keep twisting and turning.

A knife is invaluable. If you have not one, grab a rock or a handful of dirt or snow or anything and throw it into your opponent's eyes. Keep your knees smashing up at his stomach or crotch always. Grab him with Thumb-Down grips and pull him into blows. Get your feet between yourself and your opponent when on the ground.

Breathing and Sound

Exhale as you strike. In practice, growl "Rwr" as you suddenly clamp a lock on your partner, and gasp "Ahhh" as you strike. Sound is very important psychologically in fighting as evidenced by the effect of the Scottish bag-pipes and the Russian war-songs. Sound and silence both have their place.

Position of your feet

When standing and fighting, keep your feet well separated. Keep them apart.

Keep Close

Keep in close to your opponent. Push him back, off balance.

Keep Moving

When fighting, keep your body bending, twisting, and even spin around completely towards your opponent on occasion. What occasion? If he grabs you. You can often break a grip this way. If you turn right around to your right you can sometimes grab him with your left hand as you turn your back to him. Then pull him into a blow delivered with the edge of your right hand.

Direction of Blows

Remember when fighting for your life, you can hit above or below the belt. There are no rules. If he guards against blows from his waist up, hit below. If he guards himself low down, hit high. Keep bobbing up and down mixing your horizontal stream of blows with an occasional vertical blow.

Reaction Time

In All-Out Hand-To-Hand Fighting you have to become an opportunist. The more readily you can recognize an opening in your enemy's defence, caused by his ignorance or by an unexpected trick on your part, the greater are your chances of overcoming him.

You must shorten your reaction time in all the fighting methods described. At first practice the methods slowly and exactly. Gradually speed up every movement. Develop little movements and reflexes into habits, so you may act without thinking. A good Arwr man develops an automatic technique that takes care of most of his fighting actions.

Try These:
    For instance, if a man pushes you with his right hand against your left shoulder, practise gripping the cloth under his right elbow immediately with your left hand. If he pushes you with his left hand, grab at his left elbow with your right hand. Practise this until it becomes an automatic habit.
    Then after that, add further technique to the movement. Build it up. Let us add a blow. Now when your opponent pushes your left shoulder with his right hand, automatically grab cloth under his right elbow with your left hand, THEN add another reflex.
    As you grab his right elbow with your left hand, bring your right hand under your left arm to your left side. Pull him to you with your left hand grip, giving him a sharp blow with the stiffened, little finger edge of your right hand, against his right ribs. (You may give him the same blow against the right side of his neck. Strike at the spot least protected.)

* * *

    The point is to practise and develop conditioned reflexes to speed up your fighting movements. Analyze the Arwrology methods described and cut them up into individual movements which may be practiced and speeded up, then linked together.
    There are many simple "Conditioned Reflexes" like the one above which can be developed by practice. Here is another.
    "When he grabs with both hands, strike!" (Fig. 64).

Fig. 64
If he grabs with both hands—STRIKE!

UNARMED "BLOW POWER"

Why? Because his hands are occupied. He would have to let go of you to protect himself from the blow. That takes time, and if you're fast on your reflex, you will be able to get your blow in.

There is a certain amount of mental training involved in gaining the speedy reflexes of Arwrology. Don't have a one tract mind. Do not use just blows, or grips, or a particular throw. Be ready to use anything. Mix them up so that your opponent will not know what to expect.

When two men are fighting with their fists they frequently forget the use of the knees, feet, elbows and on the existence of locks and throws. Each man seems fascinated by the fighting method used by his opponent and tends to imitate it, to fight within the same rules. Do not use the "Shoulder to shoulder slug it out method". Duck down. Weave about. Spin into him. Be unorthodox.

* * *

Another reflex to develop is, *Grab, then strike.* Here's an example. With your left hand, thumb down, palm facing your opponent, grab the back of his left elbow (Fig. 65). Pull it across

Fig. 65

Pull him around by grabbing the back of his left arm with your left hand, palm facing him.

the front of him, and getting your right side next to his left side give him a hard, back-hand blow against his left ribs with the stiff little finger edge of your right hand (Fig. 66).

Fig. 66

Smash a right back-hand blow against his left ribs.

And here is a little point which any good boxing coach will tell you. If you strike with one hand, you have two things to do with the other. Guard yourself and be ready to strike a second blow.

Spinning.

Frequently it is found useful to spin into your opponent before delivering your blows. How? If you want to spin around to your right, face your opponent. Crouch down low, shoulders hunched up, shortening your neck. Bring your right arm up vertically in front of the left side of your face, and cross your left forearm horizontally in front of your right arm. Stiffen your hands out so as to be ready to give edge-hand blows. Turn your palms toward your opponent.

Now for the spin to your right (Fig. 67). Take a short step forward with your right foot. Then step your left foot far forward across the front of your right foot. Then bring your right foot back, spinning right around in front of your opponent to face him suddenly, delivering a blow with the back of your right elbow, following with an edge-hand blow with your stiffened right hand. Spin in *close* to your opponent.

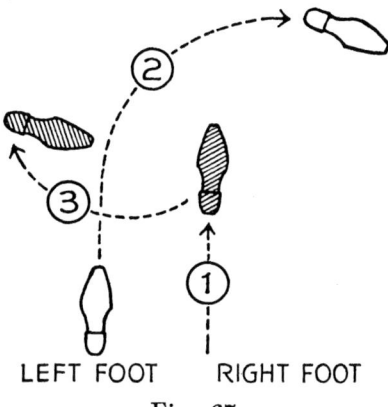

Fig. 67
The Right Spin

Then if you can get a death-dealing Arwr lock on your enemy, the rest is easy. But the problem is always how to get the lock on him. Fully seventy-five percent of the battle is *getting* a death hold. Your opponent will twist and turn and bite and kick and scratch and strike at you in manners you probably never dreamed of. Thus, one of the main features of "Blow Power" is that it acts as a speedy prelude to your holds. It weakens your opponent and helps to get him into proper position for a hold. Always aim for an Arwr lock. They are described farther on.

* * *

KICKING PRACTICE

How to Kick the Enemy when he is Down

Situation : You have succeeded in throwing your enemy flat on his face. He is probably a little dazed, but do not count on it. He may be playing possum. Take nothing for granted. Just work fast, accurately, smoothly. You may have thrown him with the Face Forward, Ankle Clamp Throw. (See Part V, Chapter 2).

64 ARWROLOGY

What then?

1.—Immediately hop to his right side, *holding him* with your right hand pressing down between his shoulder blades, your left hand forcing down against the base of his spine. Put your left foot near his right side and bring back your right foot (Fig. 68).

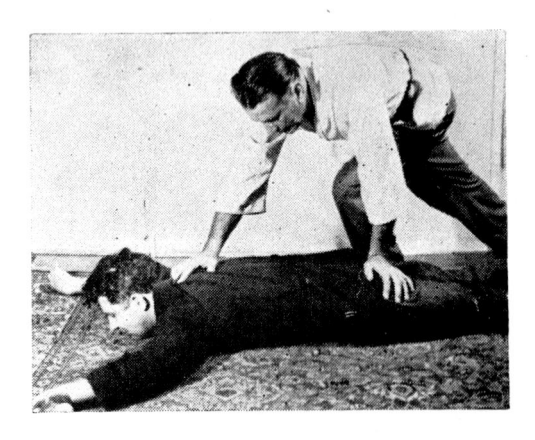

Fig. 68
You've thrown him on his face. Hold him there.

2.—Swing around to a right angle with his body so you face directly to his left and kick his right ribs with your right toe. This may result in broken ribs (Fig. 69).

3.—Then, without losing time, step your weight down on your right foot, near his *right* side, and, passing your left foot across his back, kick BACKWARDS with your left heel, striking his left ribs (Fig. 70).

4.—Again without hesitation place your weight on your left foot near his *left* side, and turning around to your left, kick down against the right side of his head with you right heel (Fig. 71).

UNARMED "BLOW POWER"

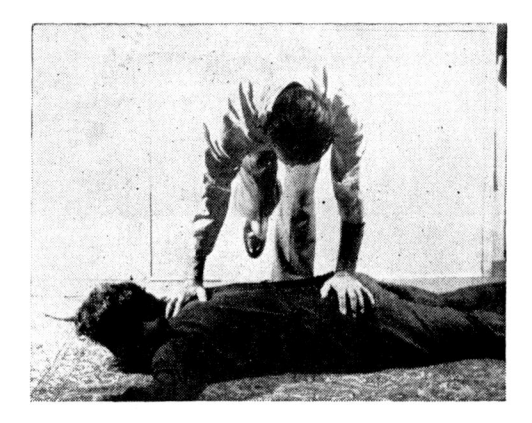

Fig. 69

With right foot kick him in the ribs.

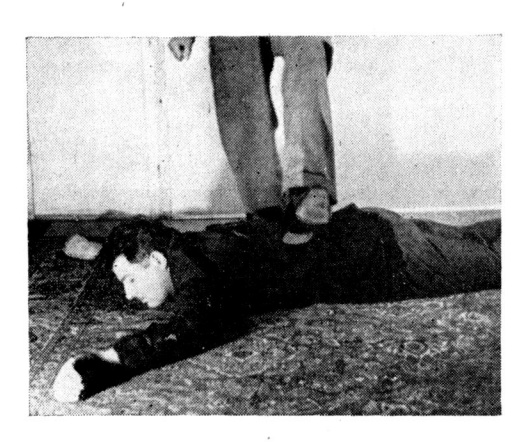

Fig. 70

Step over him and kick him in the ribs with the heel of your left boot. (Army boots have good heels.)

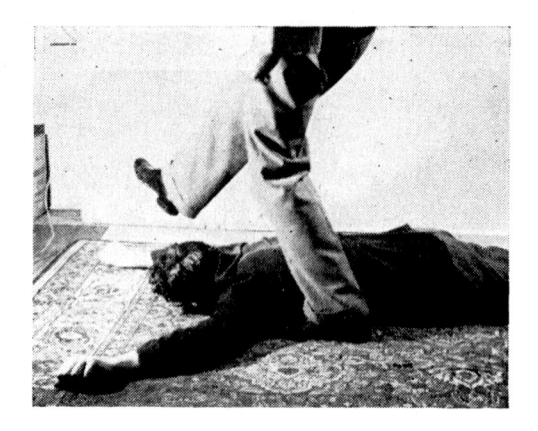

Fig. 71
Pivot on your left foot and kick him in the head with your right heel.

5.—Kick against his temple about half way between the top of his ear and the top of his forehead (Fig. 72).

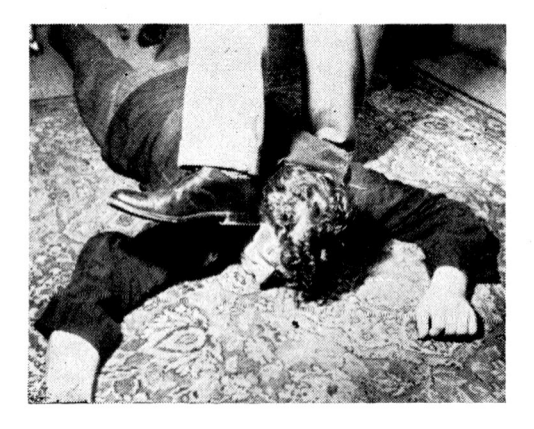

Fig. 72
Kick his temple. This may be fatal.

This location is used because you may fracture his skull here, over the region of the middle meningeal artery, which may be torn and cause death.

After you have practised this routine, practise kicking his right ribs with your right toe as in Figs. 68 and 69, but then pass your *right* foot over his body and kick back at his left ribs with your *right* heel.

Have someone read the instructions to you while trying these methods on a partner.

I cannot repeat enough the importance of being able to do these methods from either side of your opponent. Master one side first. Really master it. Then try the other side.

Jumping onto your opponent with both heels landing on his abdomen or back is a good trick, if he does not twist aside and throw you off balance.

It is generally wiser to *hold him down* until you kick him, otherwise he may grab your legs and twist you off your feet.

ADDITIONAL NOTES FROM INSTRUCTOR ON CHAPTER 4

Chapter 5

THE D-U-R-A HOLD

Duck
Under
Right
Arm

Purpose : 1. Exercise
2. Psychological value
3. Method of carrying a wounded comrade with one hand.
4. Offense throw.

1. Exercise

THIS hold provides an exercise which teaches how to attain and maintain firm, carrying balance and with it rhythm and speed may be cultivated for action.

When applying this hold correctly you should not have to use much exertion. Students will find when they are practising it, that it will be difficult at first, especially when lifting a man who weighs over two hundred pounds. That is the exercise. Once the hold is mastered, it will not matter whether you are lifting one or three hundred pounds onto your back. When this technique has been mastered with one man, progressive exercise should be practiced; that of lifting or throwing one man after another in quick succession. You may find that variations in weight and height may reveal weaknesses in your technique, which you should analyze and correct.

2. Psychological Value

This comes when one man is faced by four or more opponents and practices his speed by trying to throw them all within a definite time limit. (Seconds) A self-confidence and power of initiative is created by the habit of facing more than one man, singlehanded.

3. Method of Carrying a Wounded Man with one Hand

This hold provides a simple method of carrying a man, who weighs more than you do, on your back.

This would be especially valuable in certain instances when you might have to carry a wounded comrade back from a Commando raid, with only one arm available. Perhaps you are wounded in the other arm, or perhaps you are carrying a Tommy gun.

4. Offense Throw

Perhaps you will be able to throw one of the enemy over your head with this hold, IF he lets you grab him, IF he does not grab you about the neck, IF he does not pull back after you have grabbed him.

I do not think highly of the D-U-R-A Hold for active fighting, unless you find yourself in a suitable position for using it (Fig. 73).

There are many other throws, much more effective for offense work. Still, master it. These D-U-R-A throws *have* been used to good advantage, and the technique used is valuable in learning more advanced combat work.

THE D-U-R-A HOLD

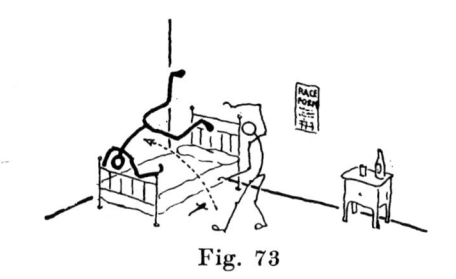

Fig. 73

Does The D-U-R-A Throw Work? It Has :

AN ACTUAL CASE when this throw was employed effectively is reported by a member of the Society of Arwrologists.

At that time he was a member of Canada's most famous police force and he had gone to arrest a suspected dope peddler.

As he entered the man's room, the man reached for a knife under the bed. Before he could grasp it, the police officer grabbed him and threw him with the D-U-R-A throw over the bed against the wall.

This was one time when the D-U-R-A throw just suited the circumstance.

HOW TO LEARN THE D-U-R-A HOLD

General Directions :

1.—Face your partner who is **NOT** to resist you at this time.

2.—Grab a handful of cloth over the centre of his chest with your right hand. Use a special grip called the "T-D" grip, signifying "Thumb-Down". How is it obtained? (See Fig. 74). (In the illustration, the men are wearing tough Arwr combat jackets for practice.)

"T-D" Grip.

A. Point your right thumb down, as though you were expressing your opinion of the enemy.

B. Have your palm face his chest. Your right elbow has to go up from your side to get this grip.

C. Now grasp the clothing over the front of his chest.

Anatomical Explanation of the "T-D" Grip.

When a wrist is bent in, the flexor tendons which clench the fingers are slackened, reducing the power of the hand to grasp.

When the wrist is straight, there is no slackening of the flexor tendons and the usual power of the hand to grasp is restored.

When the hand is bent back a little, the power to grasp is said to be augmented.

In the "T-D" Grip, the hand is bent back a little to allow the most powerful grip possible.

Furthermore the thumb is turned down to give it more protection and to allow a powerful twisting pull to be executed.

3.—Pull him to you and duck your head, left shoulder and arm, completely under your right arm, turning right (Figs. 75 and 76). Then pull him over your shoulders and raise him up off the ground (Fig. 77).

* * *

Now for some details. What about your feet? Your left foot steps across the front of his feet and your right foot pivots round to your right (Fig. 78). Bend down low. If necessary, rest your left elbow on your left knee, to help to support his weight (Fig. 76).

Mistakes Commonly Made : 1. Not keeping *close enough* to your partner. 2. You do not bend down low enough.
3. You do not pull strongly enough with your right hand.
4. With your right hand grip be sure to pull him well over onto your back, tucking your left side snugly against his groin. Your knees should be *bent* (Fig. 76).
5. After pulling him over, well over your back, with your right hand grip, straighten up your bent knees to raise him off the ground and balance him over your back (Fig. 77).

> Practise these movements AFTER you have studied them. Practise until you can throw any man on or over your back easily.

THE D-U-R-A HOLD

Fig. 74
The T-D (Thumb Down) Grip
With Right Hand.

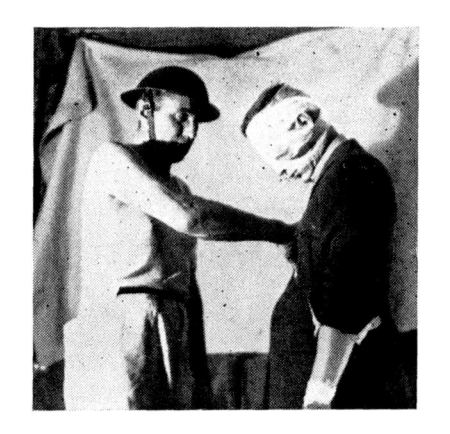

Fig. 75
Grab his chest.

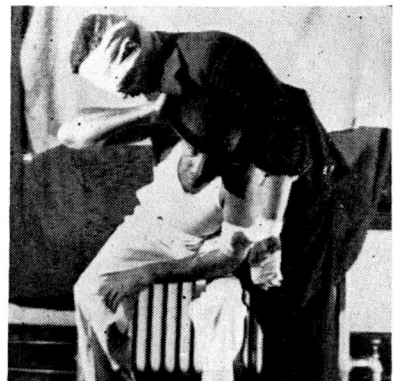

Fig. 76
Duck low under your right arm and step your left foot across the front of his feet.

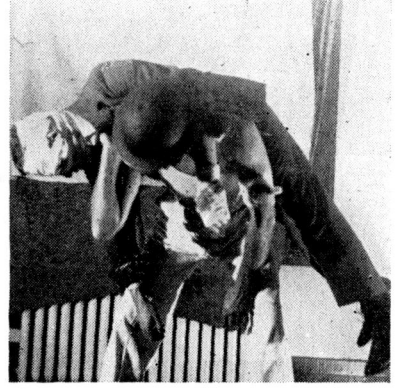

Fig. 77
Pull him onto your back. Straighten up your knees.

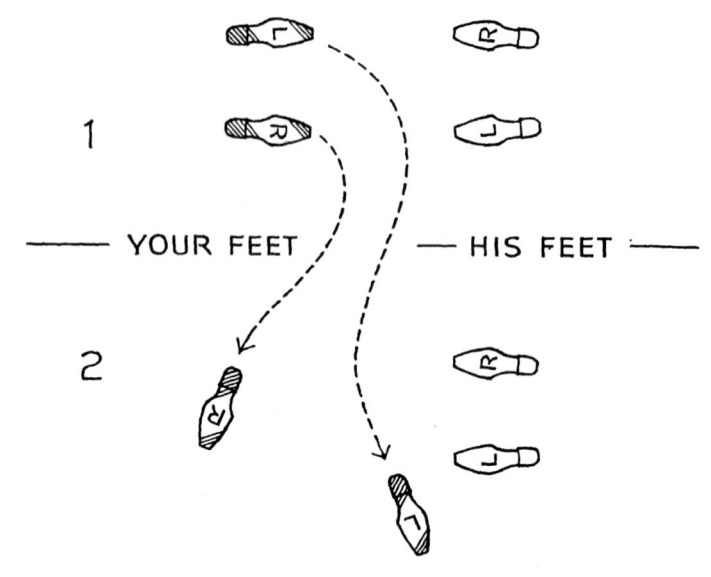

Fig. 78
Step your left foot just past his left foot.

HAVING ANY TROUBLE? HERE'S A TIP

So far you have not used your left hand. We assumed that it was wounded. But for practice and simplicity let us attempt the hold making use of the left hand (Figs. 79 and 80).

After you have grabbed his chest with your right hand, then bending down low, have ducked your head, left shoulder and arm under your right arm, now with your left hand grasp his left ankle. You are going to push it back, and off the ground as your right hand pulls him over your back.

Exactly what position does your left hand take? It is the "T-D" position again. You reach your left hand down as though you were going to pick up a hand-

THE D-U-R-A HOLD

ful of dirt. Your little finger is up, your thumb is down and your hand is twisted around so that your palm faces his leg.

Grasp just above his ankle, with your thumb on the inside and your fingers on the outside of his leg (Fig. 79), or grab a handful of cloth on the outside of his leg.

Whenever you use the D-U-R-A hold as an Assault Throw (Fig. 80), do not forget the left hand grip.

Fig. 79

Left hand grip on left ankle.

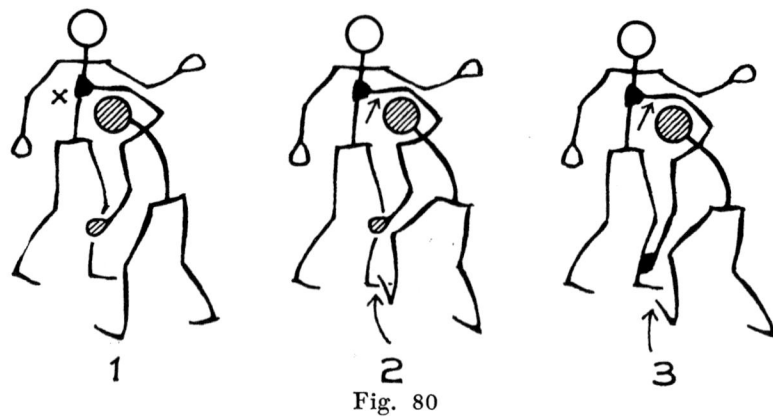

Fig. 80
D-U-R-A Hold As An Assault Throw

1. With thumb down, your right hand grabs clothing over the centre of his chest.   2. Duck your head, left shoulder and arm under your right arm, turning right, stepping your left foot across the front of his left foot so you turn your back to him.   3. Reach your left hand down to his left ankle.

Then turn your left hand around so the palm faces him and your thumb points down (T-D grip). Grab clothing over the outside of his left ankle.

Keep in close! Pull him over your back with your right hand and boost him well onto your back, so you can balance him there even without holding him. However, if he is an enemy, fling him onto the back of his head.

ONE MAN AGAINST FOUR D-U-R-A THROW
PSYCHO-PHYSICAL CALISTHENICS

By now you probably think you know the D-U-R-A hold. That is what many students presume when they have learned how to throw ONE partner. Try it against four or more men of different size.

When you can throw four men up on your back one after the other and spin around between each throw, and do all this within twenty seconds, then you are acquiring expertness.

THE D-U-R-A HOLD

In the armed forces, take four men or a squad or a section out and form a circle about one man who is in the centre. Start the exercise with four men about one (Fig. 81).

Your partners are NOT to resist now. This is to be an instructive exercise and not a free-for-all prelude to the "M.O." You may roughen it up after you have learned the throw.

Take your positions. If you are the one who is going to practise the hold, sit down in the *Crossed Legs Position,*—left foot over the right. Your four partners surround you, each about three yards away, facing you.

Here's A Rule:
> When fighting more than one opponent, always take the man on your left first.
> There are exceptions to this, one of which is when one of your opponents, not the one to your immediate left, is pointing a revolver at you. He would shoot if you do not handle him immediately. Therefore attack this man first.

From your *Crossed Legs Position* spin up to your feet in the method already described. As soon as you are standing, lunge towards the first man on your left. With your right hand grasp the cloth over his chest and throw him up onto your back with the D-U-R-A throw. Make sure he is well balanced on your shoulders. Then let him down and make a complete right spin—do all this smoothly, in one continuous motion. Take the next man. Throw him up on your back. Let him down. Spin right and do the same on each of the four men (Fig. 82).

You may repeat the cycle or work on a larger group of men. Each man should take his turn being the active, centre man.

The practise of this throw is very appropriate for half-hour exercise periods.

PRACTISE CARRYING MEN

After mastering the technique of throwing anyone upon your back with the D-U-R-A hold, practise carrying a man various distances. Try it over clear land then over rough country. Remember Commandos and Rangers! Watch your ankles when carrying anyone. Do not twist them on loose ground or rocks.

Fig. 81
Position

Sit down in the "Crossed Legs Position" surrounded by four opponents. Spin up to your feet and immediately throw the man on your left over your back, with the D-U-R-A throw.

The Geometrical Approach

After you have thrown the first man onto your back, let him down, spin around to your right and throw the second man. Spin around to your right again and throw the third man, and so on. (See Fig. 82).

Fig. 82

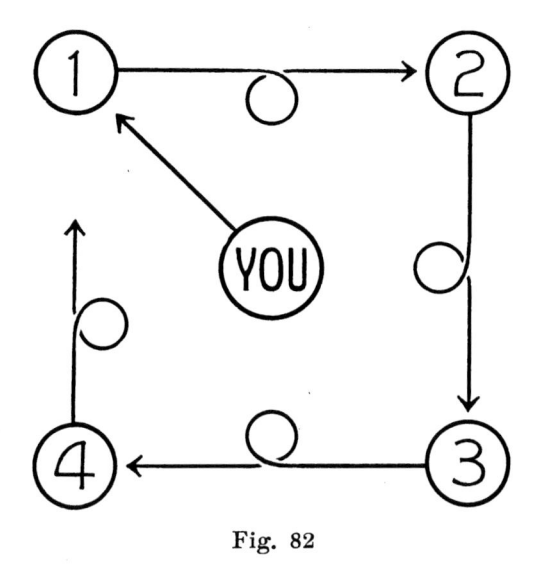

MISCELLANEOUS METHODS

The Pick Up.

There are many problems to be encountered with the D-U-R-A method of carrying a wounded man which cannot be explained in a short book of this nature. The D-U-R-A hold works best if the wounded man can stand. It is often difficult to pick an unconscious man up off the ground and put him on your back.

At first try to revive him by pressing your forefingers forcefully into the space just under the lobes of his ears, behind the angle of his jaw. Press hard. If you cannot revive him, one suggestion is to get behind him. Lift him up by gripping him under the arm-pits and boosting his back forward and up with your right knee and gradually balancing him up on his feet (Fig. 83). If you have something to lean him against, all the better. Get around to the front of him and get a D-U-R-A hold.

There is a Posterior D-U-R-A hold to be described in a future volume. The D-U-R-A hold described here is the Anterior D-U-R-A hold.

Fig. 83   The Pick Up.

OLD TRANSPORTATION METHODS
Fireman's Lift.
  Probably every boy has learned the "Fireman's Lift", in which your left hand grabs his right wrist and ducking under his right arm you pass your right arm under his crotch and loop it around his right leg (Fig. 84). Then pull him over your back and carry him away. It is moderately successful.

Fireman's Drag.
  And don't forget the trick of tying his wrists together, looping his tied wrists over your neck and dragging him face up under you (Fig. 85).

Fig. 84
The Fireman's Lift.

Fig. 85
The Fireman's Drag.

ADDITIONAL NOTES FROM INSTRUCTOR ON CHAPTER 5.

PART II
ATTACK METHODS

PART II

ATTACK METHODS

Chapter 1

ASSAULT TRIP THROW
(Attacking below the arms.)

Situation :

FACING your opponent, you rush towards him, either from his right or his left side.

Since it is generally more difficult to throw him from his *left* side, let's describe that procedure first.

Whenever you attack him from his right side with this throw, just substitute "left" for "right", and "right" for "left", throughout the instructions. You should be able to perform the throw with equal efficiency from either side.

General Instructions :

Attacking his LEFT side.

· At first, to learn this throw, face the same direction as your partner, standing close to his left side. Place your right leg well *behind* his legs, pressing the front of your right thigh tightly against the back of his left thigh and putting your right foot past the back of his right foot (Fig. 86).

At the same time, stretch your right arm out across the *front* of his body, just below his belt if possible and turn your thumb down so your palm faces him. He is now sandwiched in between your right arm across the front of his stomach, and your right leg behind his legs (Fig. 87).

> You can often throw him off balance just from here by pushing the upper part of his body back and around to your right, levering him back over your right leg with your right arm (Fig. 91).
> If you're in a hurry this simplified version of the throw may be useful. But perhaps you want to throw him harder. In that case you will have to use both arms.

Using Both Arms.

Facing the same direction as he is and at his left side, put your right leg behind him and your right arm across the front of his body as before.

Now turn your left wrist around so the palm faces *up* and slip your left arm under your right arm and *behind* his back snugly. Put your left arm well behind his back so your left wrist projects past his right side.

Then if his stomach is not too big, and if your arms are not too short, encircle his body tightly with your arms and grab your left wrist with your right hand, palms facing each other (Fig. 88).

Now lever the upper half of his body back with your right elbow and arm, and lever the lower half of his body forward with your left arm which is low across his back.

Lean a little forward, bending your right knee slightly so your right foot is firmly on the ground, and throw him back over it (Fig. 89). Turn to your right.

> Fig. 93 shows this aspect of the throw when it is performed by attacking his *right* side. After practising the throw from his left side, try it from his right side, reversing the directions. After

ASSAULT TRIP THROW 85

throwing a man to the ground, *immediately follow up* your advantage by delivering blows, kicks, and getting an Arwr lock. Don't just stand there looking at him (Fig. 90).

Although your opponent actually may be a taller man than you are, once you are both on the ground, you temporarily become equals. On the ground all men become the same height. If you're up and he's down, you temporarily have the advantage of being comparatively taller. Use that advantage.

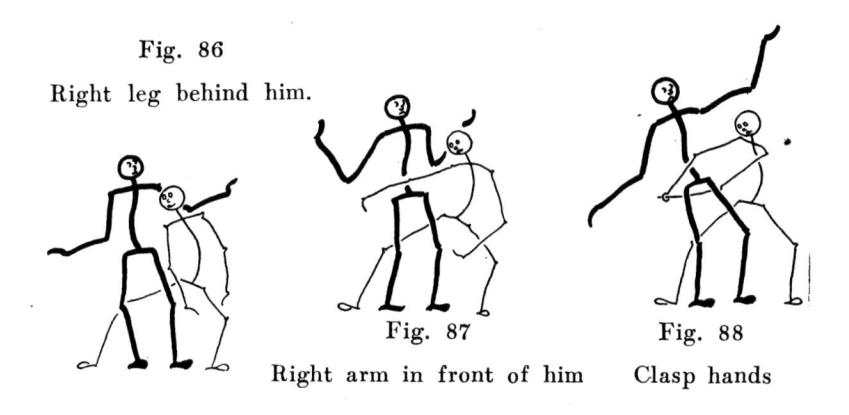

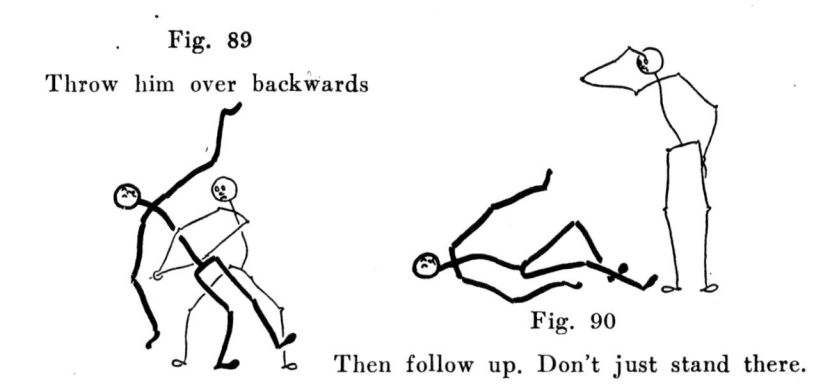

Fig. 86
Right leg behind him.

Fig. 87
Right arm in front of him

Fig. 88
Clasp hands

Fig. 89
Throw him over backwards

Fig. 90
Then follow up. Don't just stand there.

TIPS TO MAKE THE THROW EASIER WHEN ATTACKING HIS "LEFT" SIDE

1. Pick up his left leg:

When passing your right arm across the front of his stomach, be sure you bend down LOW enough. After putting your right leg behind his legs, you may often throw him easily off his feet by scooping up his left leg by passing your left arm *behind* his left knee from the outside and lifting it up high.

This puts all his weight on his right foot. Now all you have to do is to push him off balance. How?

Put your right foot snugly *behind* his right foot so he will not be able to step or hop back. Then pull his left knee up high with your left arm looped under it, and *turn sharply to your right* and trip him off his feet with your right foot behind his right foot.

2. Remember Blow Power:

At any time you may deliver a right elbow blow up into his crotch, stomach or even under his chin.

3. And here is a rule:

If at anytime you think your opponent is going to prevent you from getting whatever hold you are attempting, immediately stop trying to get the hold and strike furiously at him with back-elbow and edge-hand blows, and kicks. Often you can get a different hold. The main point is to let him reap a whirlwind of blows and kicks, and get another hold.

What do you forget about?

A man wrestling generally forgets to give blows, and a man boxing generally forgets to get holds. That is only natural from past training in "Sports". But when *fighting* for your life you must be able to mix up blows with holds, fast! A fast reaction time is of paramount importance in Arwrology.

4. What about his arms?

This throw may be applied *enclosing* both his arms within your right and left arm grip about his body, or you may enclose just his left arm when you attack from his right side, or just his right arm when you attack him from his left side. If his enclosed arm tries to pull up your encircling arm, give him a blow with your free hand (Fig. 93).

Look out for a head-lock with his right arm when you are attacking his right side, and vice versa. Keep your chin tucked in and your shoulders hunched up to protect your neck against it. Grabbing and twisting testicles can be painful enough to relax an opponent's grip, IF he does not wear too much clothing to prevent you getting the grip.

5. Follow up when he's down :

After you have thrown him off his feet, what then? He may still be able to get up and kill you. So to prevent this, after throwing your enemy, follow up with blows, kicks and Arwr locks.

——*Further Recommendations*——

"When in a fight, spin to your right".

This is a good little rule taught in the Society of Arwrologists. It is one of the many reminders to *keep moving* when fighting. While moving you are harder to hit, and it makes it more difficult for your opponent to judge when or where or with what you are going to hit him.

So by spinning around fast—once or several times—you can often confuse your opponent and get in close to him.
Keep bent forward. Press forward all the time so you can push your opponent back by the force of your onrushing spin.
Crouch very low. Lower than that! The lower you crouch the harder it is for anyone to push you off balance. Remember this. And keep your legs well separated.

Rise up only when upon your opponent. The sudden rise up and the forward momentum of the spin help to force your opponent back.

Spin to your right or left as the particular occasion demands. There are no hard and fast rules here.

Here is a good place to review the *Spin to the Feet* exercise. If you spin to your right, throw your opponent with the Assault Trip Throw from his *left* side. If you spin to your left, throw your opponent with the Assault Trip Throw from his *right* side.

Twisting and turning suddenly is another important feature

in the technique of all-out hand-to-hand fighting which cannot be over emphasized. Anyone who has tried to restrain an insane man will probably agree that the insane patient seems to have an abundance of super-human strength. This is partly because the insane man is quiet one moment and then the next moment twists and turns so suddenly and so unexpectantly and so violently that often he is able to break away from very strong holds.

So when fighting, remember to act a little bit crazy. Make sudden, sharp unpredictable turns to the right, to the left, or right around, slumping down then springing up as the circumstance demands. Complete every movement with one or more blows.

SITUATION STUDY

Figure out ways in which the fundamental principle of this Assault Trip Throw may be applied.

Try This:

For instance if a man grabs your right wrist with his right hand, you may be able to jerk his right arm to your right and up, passing your left arm across the front of his body and lever him back over your left leg which you put behind his legs,—the Assault Trip Throw, from his right side.

Criticism: But often you can't pull a man's arm out straight, especially if he's expecting it.—

That has more truth that is generally realized. The first reaction when a man grabs you is generally to pull back. Withdrawal and flexion of the limbs is a defence reaction which is developed very early in life. Touch a hot stove and you pull back your arm. Later with experience fear alone makes you pull your arms in to yourself. So when a man grabs your wrist, almost automatically you pull it back. Most of the advertised Jiu-Jitsu holds, which boast that by pulling a man's arm out and doing a little twist you break the arm, are just examples of wishful thinking. It is very difficult to break a man's arm with these holds for the simple reason that he will not let you pull it out straight.

No one method in Arwrology is adequate for any one situation. You must know many methods, enough so that whenever one fails on your first attempt, you will be able to apply immediately another method. By knowing many holds, you can develop a technique of being able to do the right thing at the right moment when complications arise. You must become an opportunist. How? By constant practice. Figure out situations where you could use the throw, then try it out with a friend. You'll learn much by trial and error, after you catch onto the fundamental points of the throw.

Variations of the throw.

As in any fundamental hold, there are many variations to the Assault Trip Throw. The method described is designed to throw an opponent to the ground with a *minimum of exertion.* Maybe you've not eaten for a week or have been wounded when you want to apply the throw. As the throw is described, as little strength as possible is required.

Lift him up and bang his back across your knee.

But if you want to use your musculature, you can, say attacking him from his right side, put your right leg behind him and your right arm across the front of him, and your left arm behind him at a lower level than your right arm. Then twist him back over your right leg.

Now to be a Sampson, lift him up towards you so his stomach faces you, then slam his back down against your right knee which you keep upright.

Sounds easy, *but* try it on a man heavier than yourself!

ASSAULT TRIP THROW

This throw can be effectively applied from either your opponent's left or right side. So practise both.

Attacking his LEFT side.

Fig. 91

Assault Trip Throw

Here you have approached your opponent's *right* side. You have put your right leg *behind* his legs and you have passed your right arm across the *front* of his body, clamping him tightly to you.

Twist him back over your right leg turning to your right. As shown above, frequently only one arm is necessary to throw him off his feet.

ASSAULT TRIP THROW

Attacking his RIGHT side.

Fig. 92
Assault Trip Throw

Here your have approached your opponent's *right* side. You have used *both* hands for the throw.

You have twisted him off his feet. How?

By putting your left leg *behind* his legs and passing your left arm across the *front* of this body, over his belt is the spot, and passing your right hand *behind* him, and then grabbing your left wrist tightly with your right hand, and levering him over backwards, over your left thigh.

Here you turn to your left as you lever him back off his feet. Lift him right off the ground, balancing him over your left leg.

Attacking his RIGHT side.

Action Photograph.

Fig. 93
Assault Trip Throw

Here you have approached his *right* side. You have put your left leg behind his legs, and you have passed your left arm across the front of his waist and his left arm.

But he has managed to turn a little to his right and to pull your left arm up. Why? Because you did not put your left arm across the front of his body down *low* enough.

Promptly you have struck up at his jaw with your left elbow and you are striking him in the crotch with the little finger edge of your right hand before throwing him back over your left leg.

MISTAKES :

1.—You did not bend down *low* enough. So your left arm went across the front of his body *too high*.

2.—Your right thumb should be tightly pressed in to your fingers for the edge-hand blow.

DOES THE ASSAULT TRIP THROW WORK? IT HAS

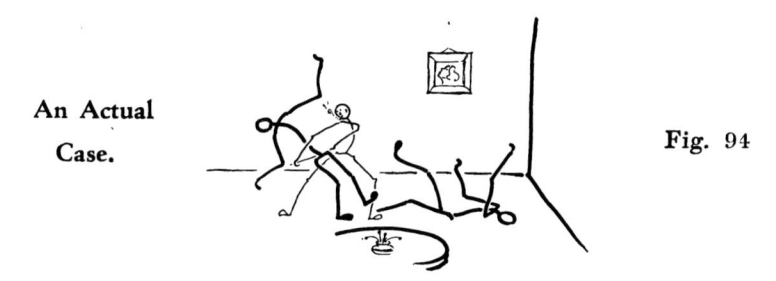

An Actual
Case.

Fig. 94

One evening in 1942, Mr. G. B., a member of the Society of Arwrologists, was quietly smoking and discussing the subject of Arwrology when two men, inebriated to a domineering degree, interrupted his conversation and started to prove in a style too rough for gentlemen that Mr. G. B. did not know what he was talking about.

To avoid personal injury and to decide the issue, Mr. G. B. rapidly threw one after the other rather hard to the floor with the Assault Trip Throw. Then he quietly finished his cigarette.

ADDITIONAL NOTES FROM INSTRUCTOR ON CHAPTER 1.

Chapter 2

STEP BACK TRIP THROW

(Attacking above the arms.)

Situation : Your opponent rushes at you.

What to do : As he comes at you lean forward and over to your left a little with your right foot slightly advanced. Be like a tiger ready to spring. Be ready to step back with your left foot then shift your weight onto it.

General Instructions : Attacking his RIGHT side.

    1.—To learn this throw face your partner. Your left hand grabs the back of his right arm just above the elbow and pulls it to you *past your left side*. (Not between you and your opponent.)

    Your left palm *pushes* forward against the front of his left shoulder (Fig. 95).

    2.—Put your right leg behind his right leg, crossing the back of your knee against the back of his right knee. Balance your weight onto your left foot, so you can take your right foot off the ground (Fig. 96).

    3.—Sweep his right leg from under him by hooking it at the knee with your right leg and powerfully pulling your right leg back to your right. *At the same time* pull his right arm to your left and down and push your right hand forcefully against his right shoulder.

Pivot around to your left on your left foot (Fig. 97).

4.— He's down (Fig. 98). Now put him out!— With kicks, blows or Arwr locks.

Step Back Trip Throw

>Your left hand *pulls* his left arm past your left side.
>Your right hand *pushes* his left shoulder.

Fig. 95

Fig. 96

>Put the back of your right knee behind his right knee.
>Bend your left knee. Sag down on it.

ASSAULT TRIP THROW

Fig. 97

Sweep up his right leg from under him by pulling back your right leg and *push* his left shoulder with your right hand and *pull* his right arm with your left hand.

(Note the automatic reflex break-fall position of his left arm—fingers out stiff and straight, and forearm and hand horizontal with the ground.)

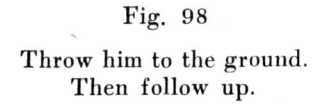

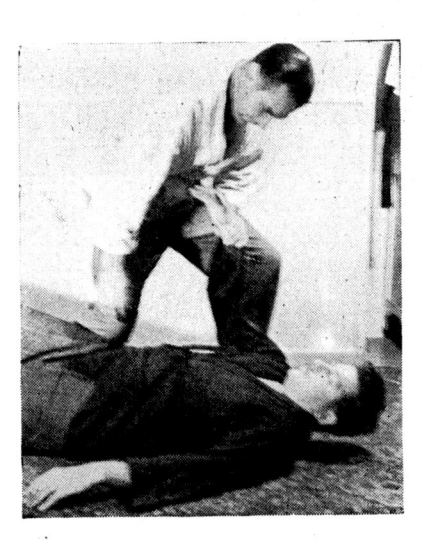

Fig. 98

Throw him to the ground. Then follow up.

(Note : Even after breaking his fall, he has kept his head off the ground —a good point.)

But what if he doesn't go down? Book no good? Frankly this throw is a technique builder. I doubt if I would ever use it. However it is extremely important because it develops essential balance and poise.

The Japanese practice a throw very similar to this, the Kekaeshi Throw, and they claim it is very practical, but I doubt it, unless several other little tricks are woven into the throw to make it more reliable.

Some Points.

If your opponent resists forward then instead of pushing his left shoulder with your right hand, jab your right thumb into the left side of his neck, or give a sharp blow against the right or left side of his chin with the heel of your right palm,—an example of combining blows with throws (Fig. 99). Push against the left side of his chest with the front of your right elbow when pushing him over your right leg.

Whenever you do not think you will be able to complete the throw, pull him towards you with your left hand grip and give him a back edge-hand blow with your right hand against the side of his neck.

This throw works best when your opponent is in motion, coming towards you. As soon as he steps his right foot forward onto the ground, that's the exact moment to put your right leg behind it and throw him off balance.

The throw has to be executed at exactly the right time. Otherwise he'll lean forward and put up forceful opposition. This throw will teach you *timing*.

STEP BACK TRIP THROW

Fig. 99

You can give a blow to the left side of his chin with the heel of your right palm instead of a push against his left shoulder.

SPEED THROW

There is a fast way to apply this throw.—

Instead of grabbing cloth, just push and pull. With the heel of your right palm give a sharp forward blow against the front of his left shoulder, and with your left palm pull the back of his right upper arm and shoulder to you. Put your right leg across the outside of his right leg and behind his legs. With a hard backward pull of your right leg, strike against the back of his knees, the right one particularly.

Do these three actions *simultaneously;*—left hand pulls, right hand pushes, right leg goes behind him.

Twist him off his feet. Turn sharply left, throwing him to the ground.

Other Variations of the Throw

To Apply the Posterior Arwr Lock.—In order to be able to apply promptly the Posterior Arwr Lock as, or after, you throw your opponent with the Step Back Trip Throw, do not pull his right arm past your left side, but pull it between you and your opponent.

* * *

Using the Hip.—After mastering the preliminary methods described, instead of putting your right leg behind the back of his right leg, you may be able to swing your right hip well behind his right hip and butt him up high as you throw him.

K. B. S. (Know Both Sides)

Again I repeat. Here as in most of these methods, after learning the throw using your right leg to trip him back, reverse the directions and put your left leg behind his left leg to throw him over, pulling his right elbow with your right hand and pushing his left shoulder with your left hand.

ADDITIONAL NOTES FROM INSTRUCTOR ON CHAPTER 2.

DEATH LOCKS

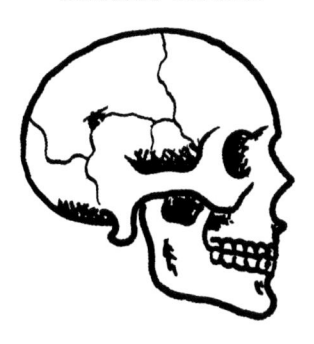

Chapter 3

NECK ROPE THROW

Purpose : To silence a sentry from behind.

Practice Position :

Face your opponent's back. Grasp the ends of a handkerchief, a piece of rope, doubled shoe-lace or cloth. Have about four inches between your hands. Not too much!

First Movement :

Stalk up behind your opponent (Fig. 101). Spring up at him slipping the rope over his head and catching him across the front of the neck with it (Fig. 102). To help bend him back slam your right knee in his back, or bend in the back of his knees with your right leg.

Second Movement :

(a) Turn to your left, slipping your right hand *under* your left hand grip of the rope, and press your right wrist or elbow against the back of his *left shoulder* to prevent him from turning to his left. You turn back to back.

(b) Pull tightly with both hands. With your left hand pull towards your left and with your right hand pull forwards, thus *crossing* the rope behind his neck (Fig. 103).

(c) Bend down very low so the back of your spine is just *under* the base of his spine. Then back to back, with your legs wide apart, throw him over your back (Fig. 104).

104   ARWROLOGY

Fig. 101

Silently stalk up behind the enemy sentry with a rope, handkerchief, piece of cloth or wire stretched between your hands. There should be about four to six inches of the rope between your hands.

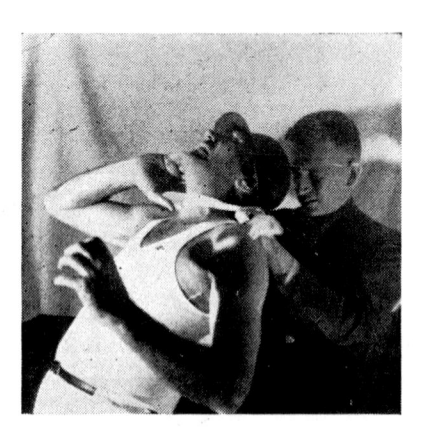

Fig. 102

With a leap get behind him flipping the rope over his helmet and across the front of his neck. Pull tightly to prevent him from calling out.

NECK ROPE THROW

Fig. 103

Slide your right hand *under* your left hand grip of the rope. Turn your back to him so your right arm and shoulder pushes against the left side of his back to prevent him from turning around to his left.

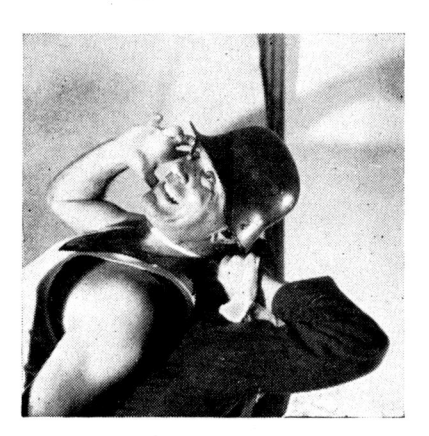

Fig. 104

Bend down low and hurl him over your back by pulling on his neck.

(This may dislocate or break the neck, so be very careful when you practise. Do NOT complete the throw.)

Tips on the "Neck Rope Throw"

Fig. 105

Note the sharp brim on the front of the Nazi helmet. Do not let the rope catch on this when you flip it over his head. If you like, you may grasp the rope in your right hand and from his right side flip it across the front of his neck, then grab the other end with your left hand.

Fig. 106

If he's very tall, push your right foot into the back of his left knee, to pull him down.

NECK ROPE THROW

Fig. 107

Get down low. Butt him low and throw him over your back. Note that your legs should be WELL separated. (You may drop down on your right knee if necessary.)

Common Mistakes:

1.—Your right shoulder is not pressed tightly enough against his back.

2.—You do not bend down *low enough* when throwing him. Butt him *low* down.

3.—You don't practice *carefully* enough. Don't tear the skin off your partner's neck. Don't complete the throw, just get the position correctly.

4.—When you flip the rope over his neck, you forget that you can bend him back by bringing up your right knee into his back or shoving your right foot into the back of his left knee. You may drop down onto your right knee, if necessary, to throw him.

After you have thrown him, what then?

If necessary, tighten the rope firmer around his neck. Remember to use back-heel kicks.

What if he grabs your wrists when you slip the rope over his head?

If he's powerful, and has succeeded in bending forward, then do not resist. Do not try to pull him back. But with the rope tightly across the front of his neck, bring your *left hand* forward across the back of his neck towards his right shoulder and swinging your *left elbow* up *high,* loop it over his head, which you push down, bending him forward. Swing yourself past his left side until you are in front of him. Now you have the rope around his neck. Force his head down with your right wrist on top of the back of his head or neck and bring up a knee forcefully to his face.

* * *

Be Sceptical

Time and space does not permit delving into all the remote tight corners in which you may find yourself if your application of these methods happens to present new problems. So first learn the classical method described, then *tear it to pieces.* In the classes of the Society of Arwrologists, we frequently have a *Tear It To Pieces* night, at which time we *try* to prove that our own methods are no good. On these occasions, we have a special open invitation for *anyone,* boxer, wrestler or strong man, who thinks the value of Arwrology is over-estimated.—Many members of the society have been recruted from strong sceptics. Enough said.

Figure out as many things as possible which your opponent could do to prevent you from completing the method you have just learned. A little heckling here can prepare you for just such emergencies.

Re-read the book with a sceptical attitude after you have practised the methods described. When you see possible weaknesses, try to improve them yourself. This will develop you more than a million words of instruction.

Ask yourself questions constantly. What if he has a gun in his right hand? What if he has a knife in his left hand? What if he is seven feet tall? (That's quite tall, isn't it?) What if he weighs four hundred pounds? What if he has a friend behind you? What if he hits you in the jaw? What if he kicks you? What if he sits down? What if he runs away? What if he breaks your first hold? Does it work then?

Figure out little tricks of your own to cover the many possible weaknesses.

One of the fundamental features in Arwrology is the development of innumerable very fast conditioned reflexes. Possible problems are studied. The defence movement for each is developed. Then speed in carrying it out is cultivated.

ADDITIONAL NOTES FROM INSTRUCTOR ON CHAPTER 3.

Chapter 4

THE POSTERIOR ARWR LOCK

A DEATH LOCK

Precautions :

BE TOO CAREFUL ! is the motto here, when *learning* this hold, which already has been referred to frequently. Practise slowly. Be sure to tell your partner to slap you or himself twice if he wants the hold immediately released, as he may not be able to call out when he wants to.

On three occasions I have seen a student, who is a medical doctor and major in the active army, faint because he tried to *resist* the applied lock and then did not have time to tap his partner. Some people are much more susceptible to this hold than others and faint very easily. So do not resist if it is being applied on you by *your* partner, but tap him twice with your hand as soon as the pressure gets uncomfortable. A sudden lurch or twist on your part may increase the pressure enough to make you faint, then and there.

What Does The Lock Do?

Properly applied, this lock can produce unconsciousness in a few seconds, if not instantaneously, probably first by pressure on the Carotid Sinuses in the neck and by diminishing the blood supply to the brain, and second by preventing breathing. Then by sudden forceful application you *may* dislocate or even break the neck.

ADVANTAGES :
    1.—It can be applied SILENTLY. He won't have time to call out for help.

2.—Great strength is NOT required.
3.—You need NO weapons.
4.—It can QUICKLY produce unconsciousness. If applied long enough it can be FATAL.

A Common Comment :

After reading the instructions for this lock, one is likely to ask: "What's he supposed to be doing while you're doing all this?"

I constantly emphasize one point. First you have to learn how to apply the hold correctly, and you'll *never* get the proper positions and technique if your partner starts to resist, twist, turn and fight back while you're endeavouring to *learn* how to apply the lock. So first your partner must co-operate with you fully, and stand still. None of this showing off and "What a big boy am I" stuff! This is a serious business and the hold is a deadly hold. If you want your neck broken, just fool around with it once too often. You get what I'm driving at. No horseplay here!

Mechanism :

Over ten years ago, when studying this hold I tried to incorporate a "Rolling Lever" mechanism, to give crushing power to the hold. In Arwrology, great strength should not be a prerequisite. If you're a gorilla, you don't exactly need Arwrology. But if you are a wounded soldier or a weakened prisoner, then you need a method of offense and defence which does not rely on strength primarily. That's where Arwrology and this Arwr lock come in.

THE POSTERIOR ARWR LOCK

A DEATH LOCK

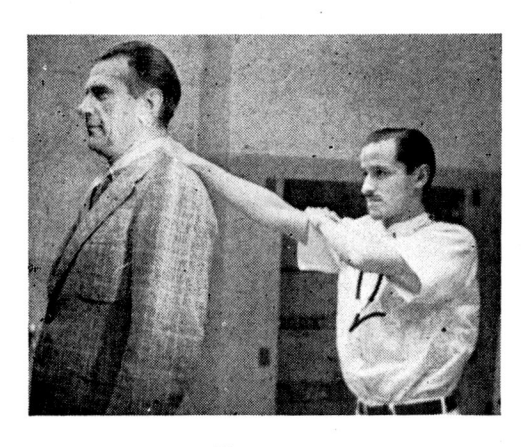

Fig. 108

In LEARNING this deadly hold,
   (1) Stand behind your opponent, soon to be one of the enemy, you hope.
   (2) Reach out your right arm, passing your right hand over his right shoulder.
   (3) Place your left hand on top of your right upper arm just above the elbow.

Fig. 109

Come in close to his back, with your right arm still held out straight over his right shoulder and your left hand held firmly on top of your right upper arm. Get this position snugly so his neck fits air-tight in the angle between your right arm and left wrist.

Your left elbow rests on his left shoulder.

THE POSTERIOR ARWR LOCK

Fig. 110

Then bend your right arm across the front of his neck under his chin. Keep your left hand grip on your left upper arm.

Turn slightly to your left so your right hip is closer to him than your left.—Turn sideways! (Beware of Kicks.)

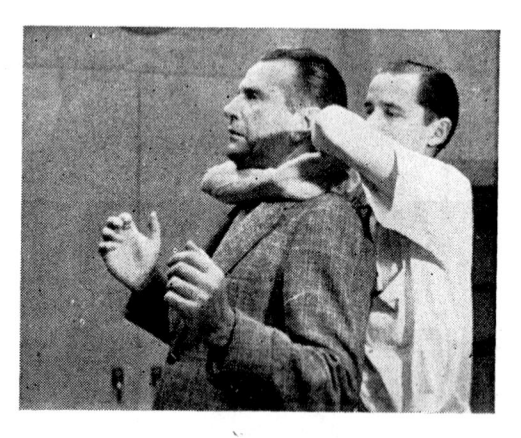

Fig. 111

Keeping your left hand firmly on your right upper arm, reach your left elbow up high, and then turning your right palm slightly forward, slide your right hand under your left elbow and forearm AND SLIP IT UP on top of your left arm as far as possible just above the elbow. To do this effectively now bring your elbows close to each other.

THE POSTERIOR ARWR LOCK

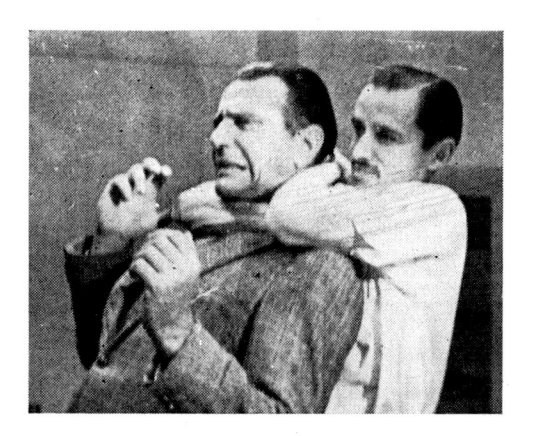

Fig. 112
The Lock.

Position of your hands.

Squeeze the lock in snugly about his neck, *first* with your wrists turned so both your right and left palms face forward, with the little finger edges of both hands *up*.

Then rotate your wrists down so your palms face down. Hug your upper arms with your fingers. Then the *thumb edge* of your right forearm should cut *up* into the front of his neck, and the little finger edge of your left hand should cut down into the back of his neck. Don't let his chin or the front of his neck get into the space at the angle of your right elbow bend.

Fig. 113

The Lock Applied.

Your left hand is kept firmly pressed on top of your right upper arm all during the hold. Your right hand is up through your left elbow bend with fingers pressing down on your left upper arm.

The lock must be clamped so tightly that there is no space *at all* between his neck and your arms, anywhere!

Pull back your right elbow. Be sure to turn the little finger edge of your right hand down. Arch up your right wrist stiffly. You are trying to cut the thumb edge of your right *forearm* into the front of his neck. I repeat—don't let the front of his neck get into the bend of your right elbow. There's too much space there.

Force your left wrist forward against the back of his neck, forcing the left side of his neck forward *to your right*. Be sure to turn the little finger edge of your left hand down. Arch up your left wrist. Force his head forward over your right forearm which you pull back against his neck like a noose.

THE POSTERIOR ARWR LOCK

Try to clamp as much of your right wrist as possible in the bend of your left elbow joint, and as you turn the little finger edge of your right hand down, lever your left forearm forward against the back of his neck, low down.

Arms vary in length, so practise slowly and carefully until you are able to get the lock snugly even if your arms are long or short.

Fig. 114

A Tip.—Push in the back of his knees.

Turn slightly left while you get the lock and use your right leg to bend his knees.—Either push in the back of his knees with your right knee (see above) or bring up your right foot and shove in the back of his left knee with the little toe edge of your right foot. This brings him down a little, so you can clamp the lock tighter.

ARWROLOGY

In the evolution of this lock, the Japanese developed a crude hold, whereby standing behind your opponent, your right arm circles about the front of his neck, clamping it, and your right hand rests on your left upper arm. Your left hand then pushes the back of his head forward. This early hold lacked many important features. It is rather easily broken.

The Posterior Arwr Lock should be applied *suddenly*, as your opponent may try to put his chin down on his chest to protect his neck.—Even so, the jaw can be dislocated first, by the lock, and then the neck attacked.

The Posterior Arwr Lock may be promptly applied after throwing your opponent with the Step Trip Throw already described.

EXTRA POINTS

Grab Cloth Variation.

You may grab the clothing over your upper arms to get a tenacious hold instead of just pressing your hands on your upper arms in the Posterior Arwr Lock.

If Fighting On The Ground.

1. *Scissors Lock About Waist.*

When fighting down on the ground you can still apply the Posterior Arwr Lock if you get behind your opponent. A good trick is to wrap your legs about his waist in a "Scissors" hold. This helps to hold him while you tighten the lock.

2. *Keep The Back Of Your Elbows Between You And Your Opponent.*

When fighting on the ground, keep the back of one of your elbows between you and your opponent so you will be able to knock him over sideways with back-elbow and edge-hand blows.

3. *Kick Him With Both Feet At The Same Time.*

If you are on the defensive when fighting on the ground, try to keep your feet between you and your opponent. Then you'll be able to roll on to your back, bend up your knees and kick out at him with both feet. When fighting very close to each other, drive your knees up into his stomach and crotch.

Often when standing up if you're pressed back by his attack you can grab on to something with your right hand, put your left

THE POSTERIOR ARWR LOCK

hand on the ground and kick him back with both feet, then go after him, attacking him from one side.

4. When fighting on the ground, keep your arms, legs, body and neck bent forward. Huddle up. Then you are in a good position to give out blows, and you are in a position which makes it difficult for him to get a hold on you.

ADDITIONAL NOTES FROM INSTRUCTOR ON CHAPTER 4.

Chapter 5

CAROTID ARTERY ARWR LOCK

Practice and Actual Use :

Here's a point I wish to make clear. When you are *learning* these methods, the manner of approach often differs profoundly from when you are actually fighting for your life. When you are learning these methods, frequently your opponent is instructed to stand still, or to keep his arms down, or not to resist.

When fighting one of the enemy, you have to expect terrific resistance, as the man is fighting for his life if he is fighting an Arwr man. Keep two aspects of the art of Arwrology distinctly in your mind. You should *practise* slowly at first against a cooperating partner to prevent injury. You should *fight* with all the speed and alertness you can muster against the enemy. And when practising, remember that two taps from you or your partner demand immediate release from any hold.

* * *

Probably you have heard the story of one of our men who had a slight knowledge of Jiu-Jitsu, just enough to know that in practice bouts if you should tap your opponent twice he should, and must, according to the rules, immediately release whatever hold he has on you.

Well, this soldier was attacked by a Japanese soldier who applied a Jiu-Jitsu strangling hold on him. Our soldier tapped the Jap twice.—He was immediately released. Then he killed the Jap.

But don't rely on such flukes. Put your faith in ferocity, speed and exactness. You can develop exactness only by careful practice.

* * *

HOW TO LEARN THE CAROTID ARTERY DEATH LOCK

General Instructions:

Here we shall endeavour to learn the hold using the right arm for the lock. Either arm may be used.

1. From behind your opponent, approach his *right* side.

> (You are just learning the hold now, so your partner is not to resist. He is to keep his arms down. He is to tap *as soon as* he feels the effects of the lock. Then you are to release him immediately or he may faint or be injured.)

Put your *left* hand on his *right* shoulder in a fatherly fashion, palm down, fingers pointing in the *same* direction as his face, little finger edge close to his neck (Fig. 115).

2. Come close to him. Reach your right arm across the front of his neck and lay your right palm on his left shoulder with your fingers pointing past his back. Step well behind him, slightly turning your back to him by turning left (Fig. 116).

Put your right hip behind him. Go up on your toes. With your left hand shove the back of his right shoulder under your right arm-pit and upper arm so your right arm is pressed tightly against the right side and front of his neck. Keep your right leg behind him, well past his legs (Fig. 116).

> (When practising, you may temporarily straighten out your right arm and press the inside of your right elbow tightly against the front of his neck, then tightly bend the arm about his neck to get a secure grip. Make sure you get the upper part of your right arm as snugly as possible against the right side of his neck before you bend your right arm. Clamp the front of his neck snugly in the bend of your elbow.
> Clamp his neck tightly so the *thumb edge* of your right

forearm cuts into the left side of his neck, and your right upper arm cuts into the right side of his neck. Straighten out the fingers of your right hand. Keep your hips well behind him (Fig. 118).

3. From behind him, with your *left* hand now shove his *left* shoulder forward jamming the front of his neck tightly into your right elbow bend. Then with your left hand, which is held *palm up* and little finger edge facing to your right, reach over his left shoulder, far forward, under your right wrist, and from *under* firmly grasp the little finger edge of your right wrist with your fingers *and* thumb. Your *right* palm faces down (Fig. 120).

It may be necessary to rise up high on your toes. Your opponent will generally try to bend forward as soon as he feels an arm across his neck so balance on your left foot and push in the back of his knees with the little toe edge of your right foot, toes pointing forward, or turn a little to the left and bend up your right knee and push the lower part of your right leg sideways against the back of his knees, bending his legs. As he sags down, pull up on his neck (Fig. 119).

Pull his head back and apply pressure about his neck. How? With your left hand powerfully pull your right wrist (a) *in* to you and (b) *back,* thus clamping your right arm very tightly against the front and especially against the sides of his neck (Fig. 117).

You are attempting to compress the carotid arteries in both sides of his neck to diminish the flow of blood to his brain. So what? This may make him faint in a few seconds. If applied long enough, it may be fatal.

Before applying the pressure, shorten the distance between the front of your chest under your right armpit and the back of his left shoulder.

To soften him up you may give a blow against the back of his head with the heel of your left hand. You may even try to pull his helmet or hair sharply back.

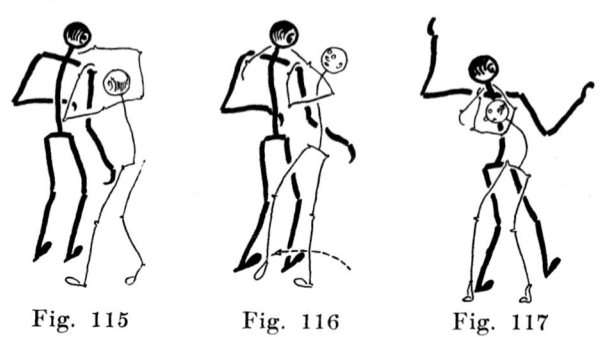

Fig. 115   Fig. 116   Fig. 117

Fig. 115.—Facing his back, from his right side put your left hand on his right shoulder. Raise your right arm. Fig. 116.—Slide your right arm across the front of his neck, resting your right hand on his left shoulder. With your left hand shove his right shoulder well under your right arm-pit. Twist left so you face the opposite direction to your partner. Put your right leg across the back of his legs. Fig. 117.—Slide your left hand between the top of his left shoulder and your right wrist and grasp up at your right wrist. Pull your right arm tightly about his neck.

At the same time go up on your toes and bump him up forward with the back of your right hip which is swung well behind him. Jerk his neck and apply the pressure about it.

IN ACTUAL COMBAT

Possible Situation

Unarmed, you wish to surprise one of the enemy by silently creeping up behind him and swiftly sending him back to his ancestors.

Modified Directions

Spring at his back, (1) putting your left hand against the back of his left shoulder so he can't turn to his left, and (2) swing your right arm over his right shoulder, across the front of his neck, into the Carotid Artery Arwr Lock position. (3) Push the little toe edge of your right foot into the back of his left knee, bending his knees. Do these three things at exactly the same time.

> Apply this Arwr lock tightly and quickly. Make certain to grab your right wrist quickly with your left hand. If you want to scare the devil out of him and don't mind making a noise, growl out "Arwr" at the top of your voice as you clamp the lock on his neck. This growl puts added force, pep and speed into the action.
>
> Use the power of sound when practising the holds. But be careful. Don't be reckless with your partner.

A TIP

If you are not fast enough, as soon as you try to apply the lock your opponent may bend forward to throw you over his head, or to twist out of the lock. That's where a powerful pull back on his neck and a kick forward against the back of his knees come in.

Always expect the enemy to resist. If he doesn't, then it's easy. If he does, be ready for him. How? By practising the holds against increasing resistance. But always be careful. Blows and kicks can help you when actually fighting.

Fig. 118

Get your hips well behind him.

Hang him with your right arm!

Clamp the front of his neck tightly in your right elbow bend *before* you start putting on the real pressure.

Fig. 119
The Lock.

Clamp his neck tightly with your right arm and increase the pressure by pulling your right wrist back and in to you. Your palms face each other, your left hand grasping up at the little finger edge of your right wrist. Place your right leg against the back of his knees and pull him over.

Occasionally practise this lock blindfolded so that by touch you may be able to apply it effectively in partial or complete darkness.

Fig. 120

What's wrong here?
It looks pretty effective.

But to be just a little bit better the sharp thumb edge of your right wrist should be turned in more against his neck so your right palm faces down. Your left hand, palm up, should grab at your right wrist *from beneath it.*

Does It Work? It Has.

An actual case.

Fig. 121

Dr. H. L. *who is a psychiatrist and member of the Society of Arwrologists was sitting in his office one day when an insane pa-*

CAROTID ARTERY ARWR LOCK

tient, a powerful sailor, rushed into the room and demanded to be released immediately from the insane asylum.

He would not be appeased and in a rage started to fight the doctor who is very slight in build.

The doctor managed to ward off blows long enough to get the Carotid Artery Arwr Lock on the man for a few seconds. This subdued the insane patient long enough for a straight jacket to be put on. Physically the man was unharmed as the doctor had applied the lock for only a short time. The doctor's shirt was torn.

ADDITIONAL NOTES FROM INSTRUCTOR ON CHAPTER 5.

ADDITIONAL NOTES FROM INSTRUCTOR ON CHAPTER 5

PART III

AGAINST A GUN

Chapter I

DEFENCE AGAINST A GUN HELD IN FRONT OF YOU WHEN YOUR ARMS ARE UP.

Situation :

You are confronted by an enemy who holds an automatic pistol in his right hand about one or two feet from your chest. You have been ordered to put up your hands.

Be Crafty. Do not raise your elbows too high. Keep your hands a little forward. Do not make it too obvious (Fig. 122). Keep your hands as close to the gun as you dare, so you will not have to move them very far when you strike the gun out of his hand.

Watch him. When his attention is slightly diverted from your hands, by a ruse such as suddenly shifting your gaze from his gun and looking intently over his shoulder with a surprised look in your eyes, then act. Do not look as though you were "Ready For Action'. Look scared, weak, but don't let him think you're going to collapse then and there, or he'll watch you too carefully. Keep your fingers tightly together.

Then suddenly

1.—Turn a little to your right pulling yourself quickly out of line of fire and AT THE SAME TIME :

2.—With palms facing you, with the little finger edge of your stiffened out left hand strike the back of his right hand about an inch up from his knuckles, knocking the gun to your left, and AT THE SAME TIME :

3.—Swing the little finger edge of your stiffened right hand up under his wrist, striking the inside of his wrist to your left. Strike at a spot about an inch above the crease of his wrist.

Your palms swing towards each other in an arc. Your palms face *you* (Fig. 123).

* * *

What will be the result? We hope the gun will be knocked flying out of his hand. This generally happens. But if it doesn't? What then?

Grip his wrist. Don't let go after you have struck with both hands. And after bending his wrist in and twisting it over to your left, twist the gun out of his hand. Quickly deliver whatever knee blows you can.

If the gun does not fly out of his grip when you strike his wrists, one simple way to pry it out of his hand is to slide your left thumb against the muzzle end and curl the fingers of your left hand over the butt end, then twist the muzzle end to your right, then in towards him and then up, over to your left, levering the gun out of his grip. Keep your right hand pressing against his wrist. Guard yourself against his left arm with your right elbow which may be raised or lowered. Be ready to give a back edge-hand blow with your right hand.

* * *

AGAINST A GUN

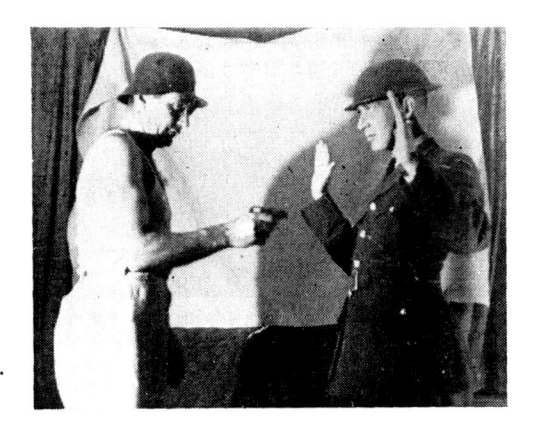

Fig. 122

He points a small automatic pistol at your chest. The smaller the gun, the harder it is to defend yourself. You do not raise your elbows too high and you keep your arms a little forward.

The closer the gun is to his body, the more difficult is this defence.

Fig. 123

Suddenly swoop down at his hand with edge-hand blows. Your right hand strikes the front of his wrist, and your left hand strikes the back of his hand. This very frequently knocks the gun out of his hand, spinning. Give hard blows. Look out for his left fist!

ADDITIONAL NOTES FROM INSTRUCTOR ON CHAPTER 1.

Chapter 2

DEFENCE AGAINST A GUN HELD IN FRONT OF YOU WHEN YOUR ARMS ARE DOWN.

Situation:

Here your opponent faces you and points a revolver at your stomach. Your arms are down.

What to do : Instead of putting your arms up as demanded, you may be able to get away with the following trick.

1.—Turn your left palm around so it faces to your left and swing up your left forearm so the little finger edge of your left wrist strikes his right wrist to your right, knocking the gun to your right. At the same time step forward with your left foot and turn to your right out of line of fire.

(This movement is very much like that employed in the "Arm Lock Against An Upward Thrust", Fig. 180).

2.—Next swing your right arm over his right arm. (As in Fig. 181). Then here's the big point. Clamp his right wrist tightly *in the bend* of your right elbow. Clamp his right wrist tightly *to you*.

3. Turn left and lever the gun out of his hand with your left hand. Give him a right knee blow to his crotch. When you've got the gun in your left hand, give him a hard right edge-hand blow against the right side of his neck.

Your left hand works on his right hand, constantly keeping the gun pointed away from you and levering it out of his grasp.

ADDITIONAL NOTES FROM INSTRUCTOR ON CHAPTER 2.

Chapter 3

DEFENCE-OFFENSE MOVEMENT AGAINST A GUN HELD AGAINST THE BACK OF YOUR NECK.

Gun At Back Of Neck

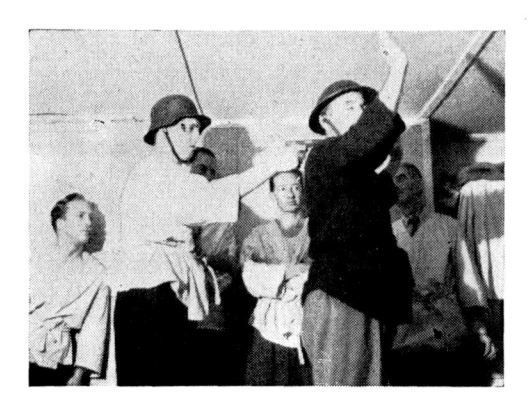

Fig. 124

What can happen?

Trying to take you as a prisoner, your enemy holds a gun in his right hand and presses it against the back of your neck.

"Hands up! March!"

(Look around a little to your right to see which hand the gun is in. Here it is in his right hand, so do this....)

Turn And Knock Gun Up

Fig. 125

1.—Turn around to your right sharply, twisting your neck out of line of fire, and at the same time :

2.—Duck down, and swing your right arm around, up, and against his right wrist, knocking his wrist up with your right wrist.

>You turn your neck away from the gun.
>You duck down beneath the gun.
>You knock the gun up.

Grab Wrist And Push Elbow Down

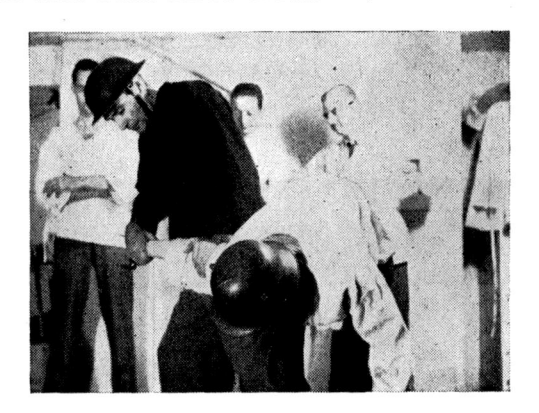

Fig. 126

Grab his wrist in your right hand and pull it down across the front of your body turning right. At the same time shove forcefully against the back of his right elbow with your left hand.

Push down on his elbow and pull out and up on his wrist.

Keep the gun pointing away from you all the time. That's rather important. Lever him down.

Lever Gun Out Of Hand

Fig. 127

You may be able to lever the gun out of his hand then and there. Holding his right wrist with your right hand, and turning right, stretch your left leg across the front of his legs. Reach your *left* hand over your right hand and turning your thumb down, and palm forward, press your thumb down against the handle of the gun. Curl your fingers over the muzzle of the gun. Push down with your thumb and pull up with your fingers, levering the gun out of his hand, directing it away from you, and towards him if possible. Now you have the gun. Then get him.

Or .... Put Him Down First

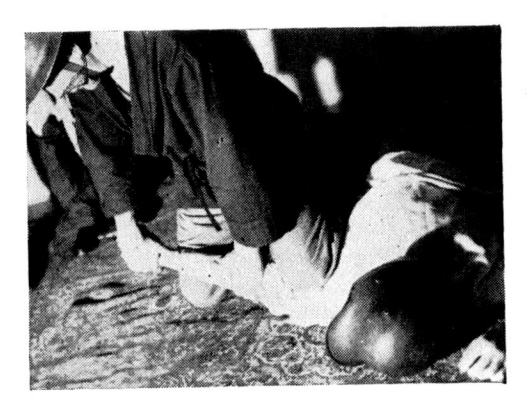

Fig. 128

Throw him forward over your left leg.

(He may try to pick up your left leg with his left hand. If he does, give him a left back edge-hand blow against the right side of his neck, (Carotid Sinus blow), as then both his hands are occupied and he can't ward off the blow very well.)

Throw or lever him forward and down onto his face, forcing him right down by pressing your left knee on top of his right upper arm. When he's down, kneel on both knees, pressing your left knee on top of his upper arm and pull his right forearm up against your right knee.

(If he bends his arm, all the better, because then a more severe lock can be applied which is described in Volume II.)

Lever the gun out of his hand as already described—turn your left hand around so the little finger edge points forward and grab the top edge of the gun barrel with the fingers of you left hand pushing your thumb down against the handle of the gun. Lever the gun out of his grasp.

DISCUSSION:
Other Methods

Arm-pit Shove.—Sometimes with the method just described, you can throw your opponent on his back by pushing the heel of your right palm forcefully up into his right arm-pit, when you swing your left leg well across the front of his legs and pull his right wrist down with your right hand. This is particularly adaptable to an opponent who is shorter than yourself.

When a pistol, held in your enemy's right hand, is pressed against the back of your *neck,* you may swing your right arm up over his right wrist, turning around to your right and clamping his wrist in your right arm-pit. Then strike him with your left hand, and putting your left foot across the front of his feet throw him over it, pushing his right elbow or upper arm with your left hand if necessary.—Danger. He may step back as you turn around.

It is not advisable to try this method against a gun pressed against your *back* as your opponent can move the gun forward and to his right at your chest as your arm swings around.

Furthermore, if you do manage to clamp his right wrist in your right arm-pit, he may be able to put the gun into his other hand and shoot you. Watch out for this.

ADDITIONAL NOTES FROM INSTRUCTOR ON CHAPTER 3.

Chapter 4

DEFENCE-OFFENSE MOVEMENT AGAINST A GUN POINTED AT YOUR BACK.

Possible Situation:

Having landed in enemy territory, you are captured by one of the enemy who points a revolver at your back.

"Hands up. March!"

Now don't raise your elbows up too high, or they will have to move too far when you go into action. Cautiously turn your head slightly to see which hand he is holding the gun in *now*. It's in his right hand in this instance (Fig. 129). You should turn your head just for a second.

Suddenly swing around to your right, swooping your right hand down and knock his right wrist across the front of his body with the little finger edge of your right wrist. Your hand points down, the back of your hand to him (Fig. 130). Simultaneously swerve sideways out of line of fire and knock the gun to his left.

Then facing him on his right as you push his right wrist to his left, loop your forearm up under his right wrist and clamp his wrist tightly in the bend of your right elbow. Twist right, yanking his right arm out. (Generally difficult). This may be facilitated by pushing against the back of his right elbow with your left palm. Stretch your left leg across the front of his legs forcing him over it (Fig. 131).

148   ARWROLOGY

Give a hard blow against the right side of his neck with the little finger edge of your left hand (Fig. 132). Then lever the gun out of his hand with your left hand.

Fig. 129

Do not raise your elbows too high.
Cautiously see which hand the gun is in.

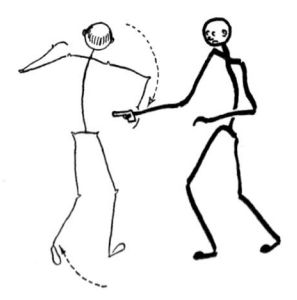

Fig. 130

Spin around to your right, lunging towards him in case he steps back, striking down and to your right with the little finger edge of your right wrist against his right wrist, knocking the gun to his left.

Fig. 131

Having turned right, and having swung your right wrist down across the front of his body, knocking the gun away to his left, wrap your right arm up around his right wrist, clamping it tightly in your right elbow bend and swing your left leg across the front of his legs. Force him down by pressing your left hand against the back of his right elbow and upper arm.

Fig. 132

Clamping his right wrist tightly in the bend of your right elbow so that the gun is useless, give a hard blow against the right side of his neck (Carotid Sinus) with the stiff edge of your left hand. Pull him into the blow. Give as many blows as you like, but fast, as chances are he'll try to pick up your left leg. Finally, lever the gun out of his hand with your left hand.

* * *

A fast modification of this defence is to turn right knocking the gun aside (Fig. 133), and clamping his right wrist in your right elbow bend (Fig. 134), then sock him in the jaw or behind the ear with your left fist as you shoot your left leg across the front of his feet (Fig. 135). Then lever him over it, turning right and pulling his right arm across the front of your body. Lastly, lever the gun out of his hand with your left hand.

> (Instead of striking him in the jaw with your left fist, occasionally it is effective to jab your stiff finger tips up under his jaw into the sensitive submaxillary glands.)

AGAINST A GUN

DISCUSSION

If you are holding a gun at a captive's back, there are several tricks which you may employ.

If he has seen you holding the gun in your right hand, then when his back is turned put the gun in your left hand.

If it is necessary to press the gun into his back, change hands without him knowing it, or substitute the knuckle of your left forefinger into his back for the gun and hold the gun at your right hip. Back up if he turns.

Fig. 133

As you turn right and swing your arm down against his wrist, stiffen your fingers out straight and strike the back of his wrist with your forearm.

The closer he holds the gun to his hip, the more difficult will it be to knock the gun aside.

Furthermore, if he anticipates such a movement, he may step back as you turn. You have to take a chance. Your own ferocity and initiative will often make a certainty out of an apparently doubtful risk.

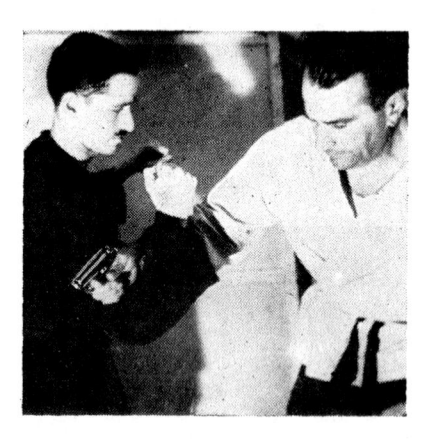

Fig. 134

As you complete your right turn, facing him, bend up your right arm tightly clamping his right wrist in your right elbow bend. Instead of pushing the back of his right elbow with your left hand, you may close your left fist and aim a blow at his jaw.

Fig. 135

Shoot out your left leg across the front of his feet. Twist farther right and strike him in the jaw to straighten his right arm across the front of your body.

Then you may give some subduing edge-hand blows, and twist the gun out of his hand with your left hand.

DISCUSSION :

Other Methods

Old methods of dealing with a gun pointed at you from in front include pushing the gun *up* to one side or the other and twisting it out of his hand. Easy said.

An old trick which is employed against a man holding a gun in his right hand at your back is to turn around to your *left*, swinging your left arm up over his arm and clamping his right wrist in your left arm-pit, striking him in the jaw with your right fist—if he does not shoot you first.

In Volume II methods are described whereby an opponent's gun or knife is twisted towards him and used against him while still in his hand.

ADDITIONAL NOTES FROM INSTRUCTOR ON CHAPTER 4.

PART IV

THE DAGGER

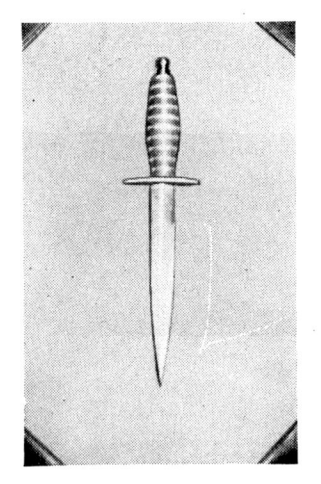

Fig. 136

The "Arwr" Dagger

This sturdy dagger was recently designed by the Society of Arwrologists for All-Out Hand-To-Hand Fighting. It features a steel knob at the end of its long handle, which projects beyond the gripping hand, and which can crush a skull in a back-hand blow. The wide handle permits a firm, powerful grip, and the knife "rides" snugly in the hand. It has a seven and a half inch blade, hollow ground, with two cutting edges, the lower two thirds being razor sharp. The proximal third has an edge designed for rough hewing. It has a tapering needle point, which is not brittle. It is balanced for throwing. It may be concealed.

Chapter 1

HOW TO ATTACK WITH A COMMANDO DAGGER

THE LEFT ELBOW LEAD

In close fighting, one of the most effective methods for attacking with a dagger is as follows :

Holding the dagger in your right hand, blade upward, bend your left elbow over the dagger, to make interference (Fig. 137).

Your left arm serves
1. To conceal the dagger.
2. To push your opponent's arms up out of the way.
3. To strike him with elbow or edge-hand blows.
4. To guard yourself.

Helpful Hints :

Crouch low. Keep good balance, feet apart. Always keep the knife moving. Watch out for his feet, arms, head or a sudden turn. Remember that he may have a knife, gun or hand-grenade.

Blind Practice :

Practise these methods blindfolded, or in the dark, after you have mastered them. This will help to give you the "feel" of an opponent. It helps to quicken your reflexes, but be very careful.

In the following methods, it is assumed that there is only one dagger. Either you have it, or your opponent has it. Make sure he is the one who gets it.

The Left Elbow Lead

Fig. 137

Hold the knife tightly in your right hand which is pressed against your stomach. Your right elbow is held close to your body.

Keep a bent left elbow over the blade. Use your left hand to ward off blows, to push his arms away, to strike him or to pull him *into* the dagger. Always try to pull your enemy into the dagger as you thrust at him. Thrust up. As you thrust, turn the blade horizontal. (Here it is vertical for visibility).

HOW TO ATTACK WITH A COMMANDO DAGGER

SURFACE ANATOMY

Where to stab the enemy:

Generally you have not time to choose a choice spot. Fundamentally there are two things to aim at to make a stab wound quickly fatal. 1. A large artery. 2. One of the vital organs in the body.

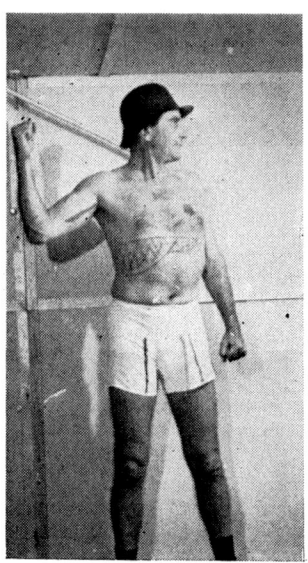

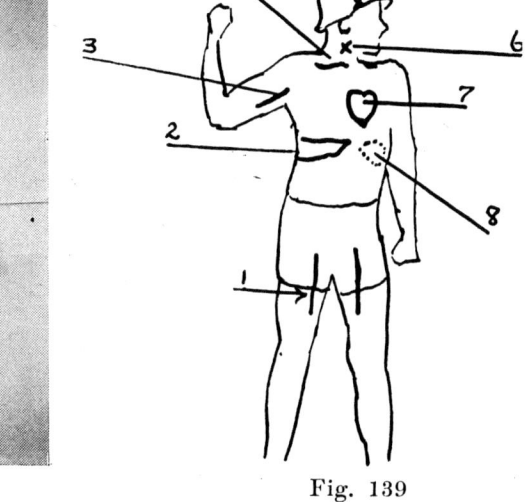

Fig. 138   Fig. 139

1.—*Stab.* Femoral artery, in inside of thigh.
2.—*Stab.* Liver, on right side behind lower ribs.
3.—*Stab.* Brachial artery, inside of upper arm.
4.—*Stab.* Down in the angle between his neck and the back of his collar bone.
5.—*Blow.* Temple. About an inch above and in front of the top of the ear. Middle meningeal artery.
6.—*Stab.* Carotid artery. Side of neck to the front.
7.—*Stab.* Heart. Left side of chest. Between breast bone and left nipple.
8.—*Stab.* Spleen. On left side of his back, behind his lower ribs.

160   ARWROLOGY

There are three main arteries. 1. The femoral in the inside of his thigh. 2. The brachial in the inside of his upper arm. 3. The carotid in the side of his neck.

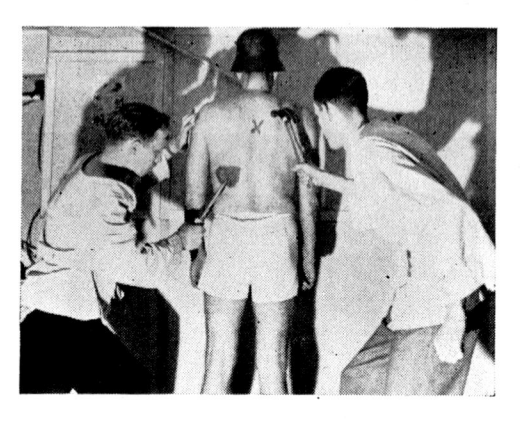

Fig. 140

1.—*Stab*. His spleen, on his left side behind his lower ribs,

2.—*Strike*. Back of his neck just under his head.

3.—*Strike*. His spine between his shoulder blades.

4.—*Stab*. His liver, on his right side behind his lower ribs.

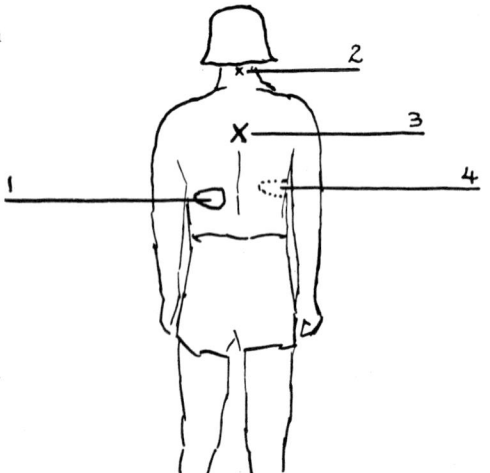

HOW TO ATTACK WITH A COMMANDO DAGGER 161

To learn the exact location of these large blood vessels consult a good anatomy book. Feel for them on your own body. Arteries pulsate, they beat like your heart.

Three vital organs which you may stab at are the heart, the liver and the spleen. You generally hit the heart stabbing in the left side of his chest between his breast bone and left nipple. Stab up under his lower right ribs to get his liver. His spleen is behind his lower ribs (9, 10, 11) on the left side of his back.

"EN PASSANT"

An interesting anecdote of the first world war was related by Dr. Fraser B. Gurd one evening to the Society of Arwrologists. We had been reviewing the military methods of stabbing with dagger and bayonet.

Dr. Gurd told of a German prisoner who had received more than one hundred and twenty-seven bayonet wounds, yet the prisoner was able to report for questioning, in three days!

The German had been knocked unconscious. A British captain had lifted him over his shoulder to carry him back to a dressing station, when the German reached down, pulled out the captain's revolver and shot him dead.

Several Irish "Tommies" who were following in the rear, saw what happened, and, in blind rage, attacked the German with their bayonets before he could fire the revolver again. Not one of the hundred and twenty-seven bayonet wounds were serious. They had missed every vital structure.

The moral of the story is that there are very few spots in the body where a stab wound is quickly fatal. Where are they? Remember?

ADDITIONAL NOTES FROM INSTRUCTOR ON CHAPTER 1.

Chapter 2

HOW TO USE A DAGGER

In the following six movements, you hold the dagger in your right hand.

No. 1

DEFENCE-OFFENSE MOVEMENT AGAINST A TWO HAND DOWNWARD GRIP ON YOUR RIGHT WRIST.

"THE CHANGE HANDS"

Here is an absurdly simple Defence-Offense movement. Holding a dagger in your right hand, with the blade pointing up, you stab up towards your enemy.

But he grabs down on your right wrist with both hands (Fig. 142).

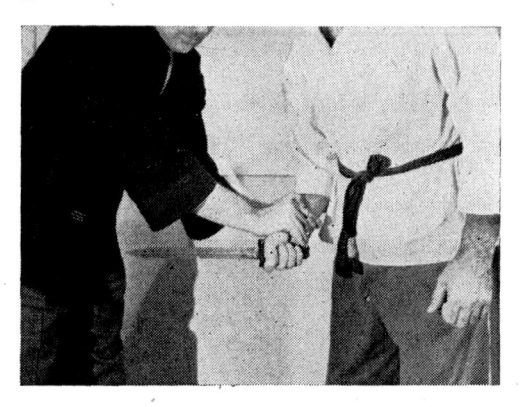

Fig. 142

You stab up at him with your right hand, and he grabs your wrist with both hands. What are you going to do?

What are you going to do now?

Just put the dagger in your other hand (Figs. 143 and 144). And let him have it! (Fig. 145).

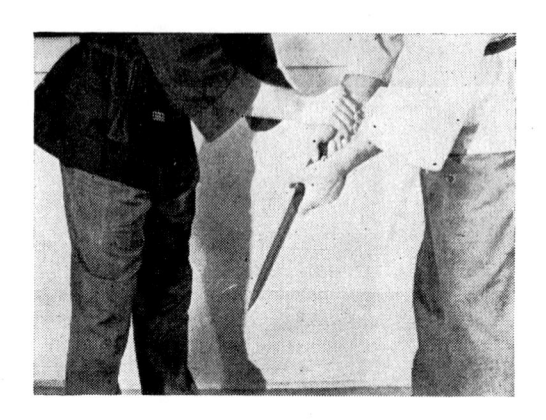

Fig. 143

Just change hands! Slip the knife into your left hand,

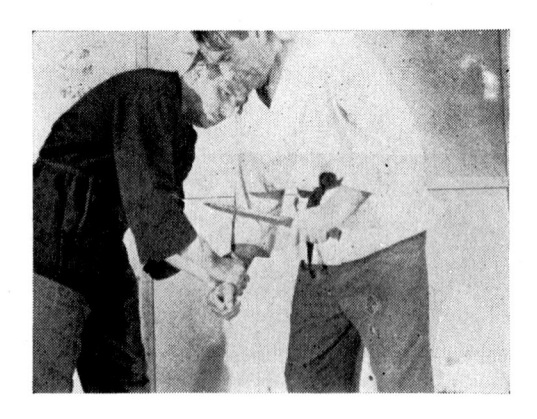

Fig. 144
—and—

HOW TO USE A DAGGER

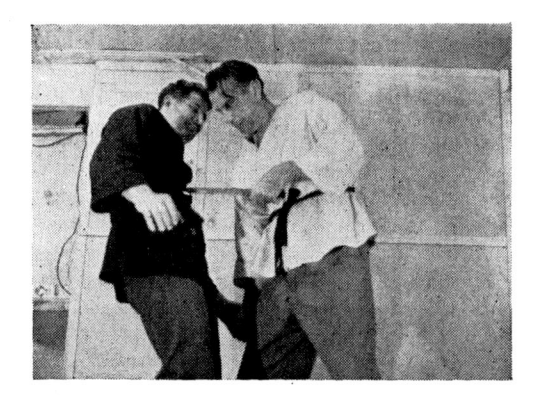

Fig. 145
stab him.

* * *

This action is simple, but it must be fast, automatic, a conditioned reflex. When fighting fiercely for your life, you have not got much time to think and the more automatic movements and reactions you have prepared for your defence, the safer will be the result.

* * *

This procedure works just as well if you are stabbing *down* at him.—Also if you have a gun, club, sock full of dirt or a rock in your hand instead of a knife!

No. 2

"DEFENCE-OFFENSE MOVEMENT WITH BLOWS" AGAINST A RIGHT HAND DOWNWARD GRIP ON YOUR RIGHT WRIST

Situation:

1.—Facing your enemy, and holding your dagger *upright* in your right hand, you have stabbed *up* at him.

2.—To defend himself, he grabs down on your right wrist with his right hand, fingers over the inside of your wrist. What are you to do? (Fig. 146).

3.—With your left hand grab his right wrist with your fingers going over the top of his wrist. Pull it down to your left pushing your right hand forward, swinging your right hand around to your left, passing your thumb over the back of your left hand. You may raise up your right elbow and powerfully lever your knuckles down against his right wrist. Pull your right hand out of his grip (Fig. 147).

4.—Still holding his right wrist with your left hand, swing your right elbow around to your left (Fig. 148).

5.—Then slam the back of your right elbow against the right side of his neck (Fig. 149).

6.—Follow up with a right back-hand blow against the same spot on the right side of his neck. Strike with the end of the handle (Fig. 150).

It is for a situation like this that the long handle of the Arwr dagger was designed.

HOW TO USE A DAGGER

7.—You may slice the dagger across the same spot on the right side of his neck. Then come back and jab up into the left side of his neck, trying to sever the carotid artery (Fig. 151).

> You may not be able to use all of these points but you should succeed in at least one or two.—Enough to count.

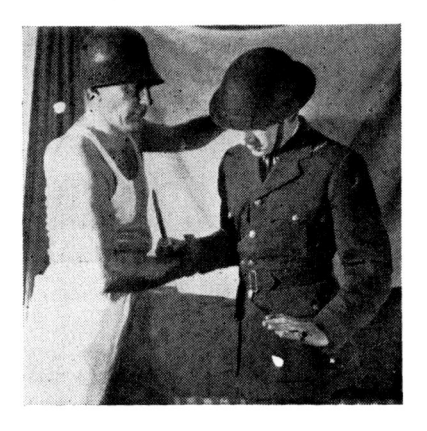

Fig. 146

You have stabbed up at your enemy with the dagger held in your right hand, blade up. He has managed to grab down on your right wrist with his right hand.

What about his left hand? It is UP to no good.

168   ARWROLOGY

Fig. 147

Your left hand quickly grabs his right wrist and jerks it inward and to your left. At the same time, push your right wrist forward and slightly to your left, levering against his thumb and getting out of his grip.

Look at his left arm. It is still up. Remember your opponent has two hands.

HOW TO USE A DAGGER

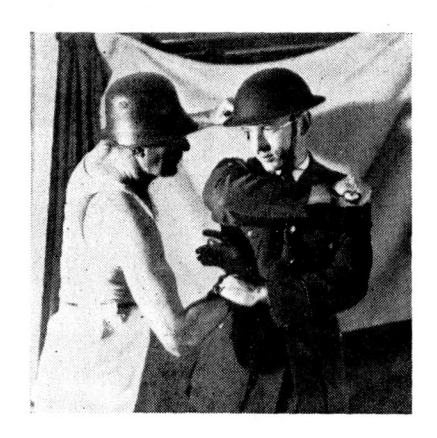

Fig. 148

Instead of stabbing his throat immediately, you may try out a little "blow power" first.

Swing your right arm well around to your left. Keep your left hand grip on his right wrist.

> (His left hand is still up. These are only photographs. In actual combat, if you forget about his left hand you mightn't be up. Be ready to guard against, or duck under, a blow from his left hand.)

170   ARWROLOGY

Fig. 149

Slam the back of your right elbow against the right side of his neck. *Pull* him into the blow with your left hand grip on his right wrist.—This also helps to prevent him from guarding against the blow.

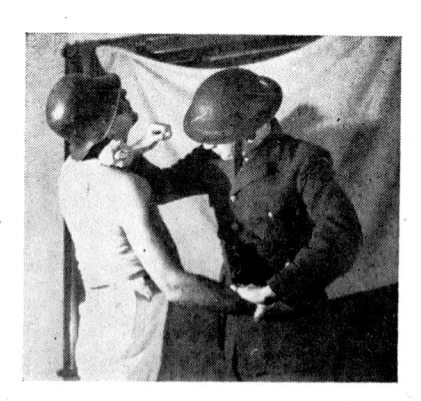

Fig. 150

Follow this up with a sharp back-hand blow against the side of his neck with the end of the handle of the dagger.

HOW TO USE A DAGGER

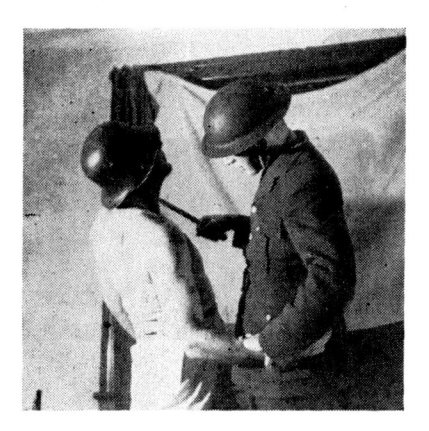

Fig. 151

Then cut across this tender area. Then jab back into the left side of his neck (Carotid artery).

No. 3

"SNAP OFF" DEFENCE-OFFENSE MOVEMENT AGAINST A RIGHT HAND DOWNWARD GRIP ON YOUR RIGHT WRIST.

Situation:

Here the dagger is held in your right hand, with the blade pointing up. The thrust is up at him. *But* his right hand grabs *down* on your right wrist (Fig. 152).

What to do:

Bend back your right wrist slightly, away from his right wrist, so you may insert your left, "stiffened" wrist in *tightly* between your bent back right hand and his wrist (Fig. 153).

Now lever your right fist in *against* your left wrist, which in turn prys his right hand grip off your right wrist (Fig. 153). You must raise your right elbow to do this. (Look out for his left fist.)

As soon as you snap your right hand out of his grip, stab him (Fig. 154).

Stab him hard. Pull him into the thrust (Fig. 155).

HOW TO USE A DAGGER 173

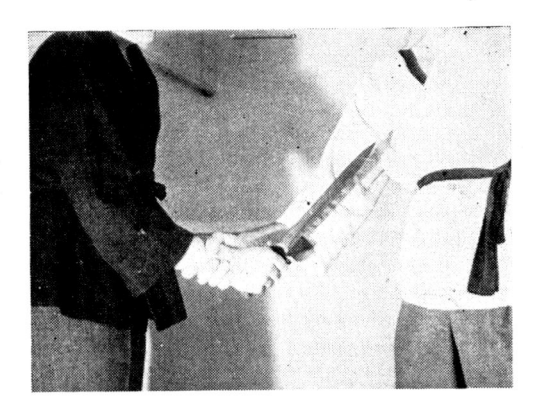

Fig. 152

You thrust up at him, but he has grabbed down with his right hand on the inside of your right wrist, thumb on top.

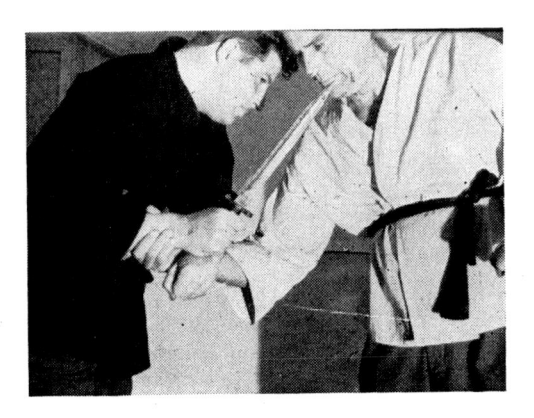

Fig. 153

Lean forward, and bending back your right wrist insert your left wrist snugly in between your right hand and his wrist.

174   ARWROLOGY

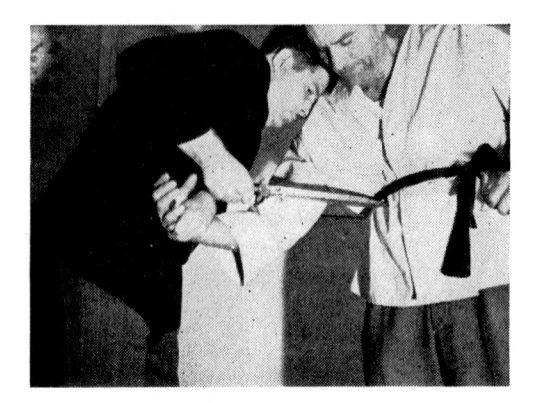

Fig. 154

Raise your right elbow and lever your right fist down against your left wrist and fist which in turn pry his right hand down, off from your right wrist. Push down with your left elbow and forearm. Lean forward. Snap your right hand out of his grip and use this sudden forward momentum to jab the dagger into him. Pull his right hand to you with your left hand.

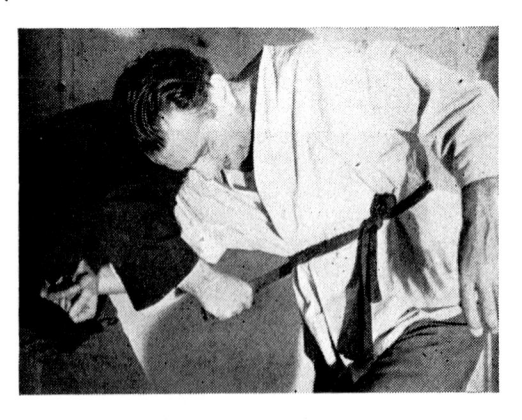

Fig. 155

Stab hard! (His liver in on his right side.)

No. 4

DEFENCE-OFFENSE MOVEMENT AGAINST A LEFT HAND DOWNWARD GRIP ON YOUR RIGHT WRIST

The dagger is held in your right hand, blade pointing up.

Preface: All the methods described may be easily divided into several definite individual movements, suitable for giving as commands to a large number of men, practising simultaneously.

The instructor may stand before his men, with a partner for demonstration, and explain each command as follows:

In this situation, you hold the dagger in your right hand, with the blade pointing up. Your opponent is standing in front of you. You have made a jab up at his body. *But* his left hand has grabbed down on your right wrist in a strong grip. What can you do?

What can you do so quickly that he cannot strike you with his free hand, his knees, or his feet?

Remember the rule: If anyone can *see* what you're doing, you're not doing it fast enough.

●

Take, POSITION! (This means that the knife is held in your right hand, blade up, and his left hand grabs down on your right wrist.)

Now, WRIST GRIP! (This means that your left hand goes under the dagger and down on his right wrist, tightly (Fig. 156). Your left elbow may be raised or lowered to guard your head or body against blows from his right hand. Beware of an unprotected crotch.)

Next, DEFENCE! (This means that you hold his left wrist absolutely still with your left hand and you jerk your right hand up and back against his thumb, lowering your right elbow (Fig. 157). This is the lever-out movement.)

Now, OFFENSE! (That is the stab movement. Holding your left elbow tightly to your body, and yanking his left arm up to your left, thrust forward with the dagger to his heart. Press your body behind the knife to give additional force (Fig. 158).

* * *

Practise slowly at first, then develop speed after you have mastered accuracy. Practise under the orders of

1.—Position
2.—Wrist Grip
3.—Defence
4.—Offense.

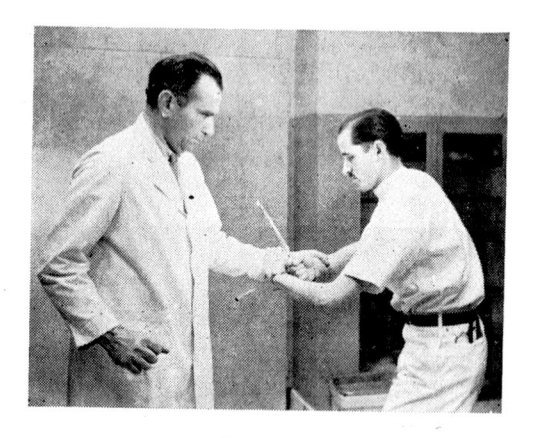

* * *

Fig. 156

Wrist Grip

Holding the dagger up in your right hand, his left hand has grabbed down on the outside of your right wrist.

Now your left hand has just grabbed down on his wrist, under the knife blade, with your fingers curling over the top of his wrist.

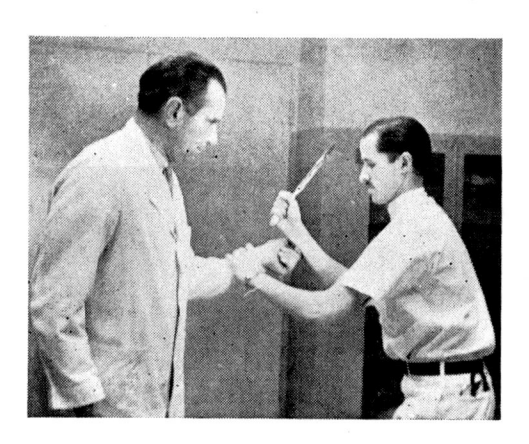

Fig. 157

Defence

With left hand holding his left wrist motionless, snap up your right hand *against his thumb* and lower your right elbow, getting out of his grip.

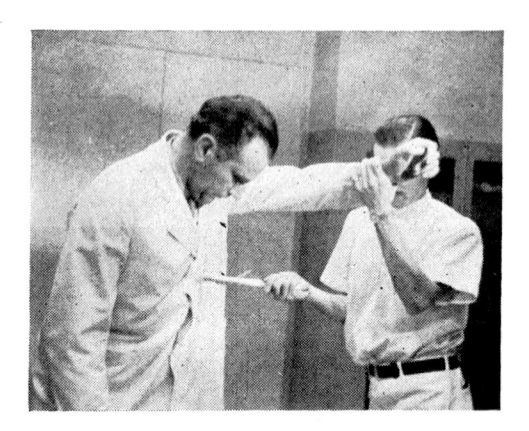

Fig. 158

Offense

Jerk his left arm up to your left, and stab him in the front of his chest, over the heart, thrusting under his arm, pulling him into the thrust.

Note that your right elbow is held tightly to your right side and you push your whole body towards him—not just a feeble thrust. When stabbing forward put your elbow in front of your hip, and drive your weight behind the thrust.

No. 5

"ELBOW SWING"
DEFENCE-OFFENSE MOVEMENT AGAINST A "RIGHT" HAND UPWARD GRIP ON YOUR RIGHT WRIST

The dagger is held in your right hand, *pointing down*.

Situation:

Here with the knife held in your right hand you have stabbed down at his heart, BUT he has grabbed *up* at your wrist with his *right* hand.

Instructions:

1.—Immediately push up under his right elbow with your left palm (Fig. 159). To add power, you may put your left elbow on your left hip.

2.—Force his elbow over to your right, and pull your right hand down, under your left arm (Fig. 160).

3.—Pull out of his grip on your wrist and stab him in the back (Fig. 161). You stab under your left arm.

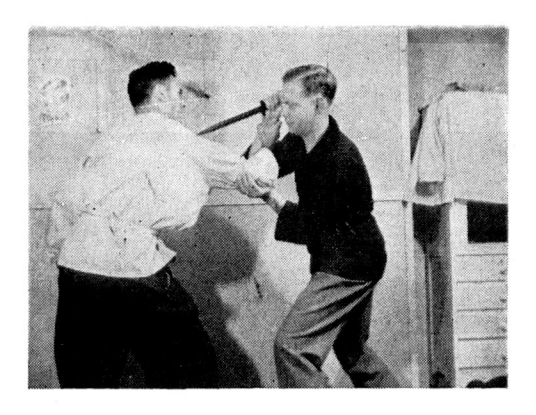

Fig. 159

As you stab down with your right hand, he has grabbed up at your wrist with his right hand. Immediately push his right elbow up with your left hand.

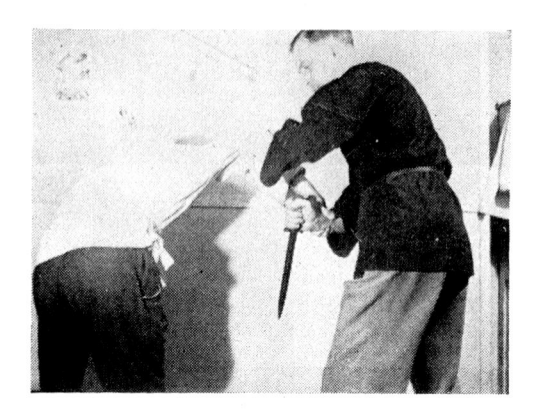

Fig. 160
Push his elbow over to your right and tug your right hand *down* under your left arm.

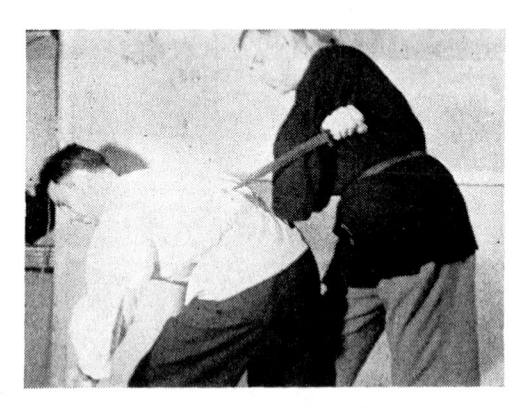

Fig. 161
Pull out of his grip on your wrist and stab him in the back.

HOW TO USE A DAGGER

No. 6

"ELBOW SWING"
DEFENCE-OFFENSE MOVEMENT AGAINST A "LEFT" HAND UPWARD GRIP ON YOUR RIGHT WRIST

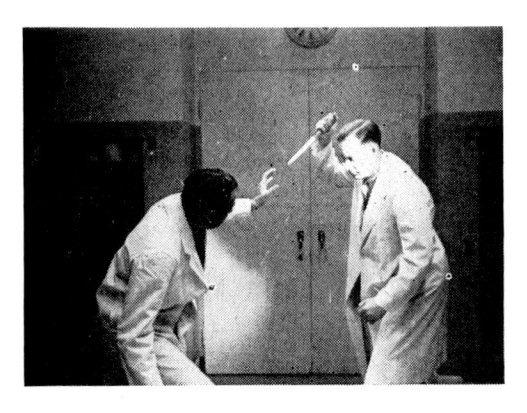

Fig. 162

You stab *down* at your enemy with the dagger held in your right hand, blade *down*.

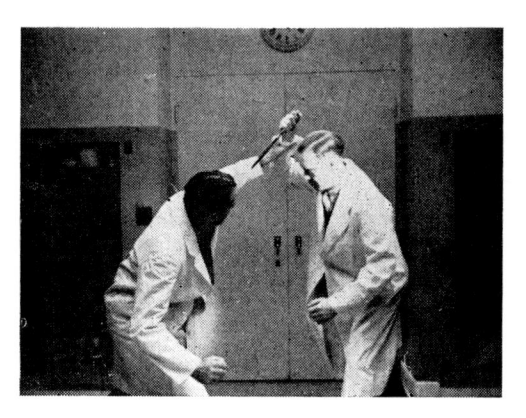

Fig. 163.

With *left* hand he manages to grab up at your right wrist. Pull back a little.

Fig. 164

Swing your right hand down to your left between you and your opponent, past his left side, reaching your left hand out towards the back of his left elbow.

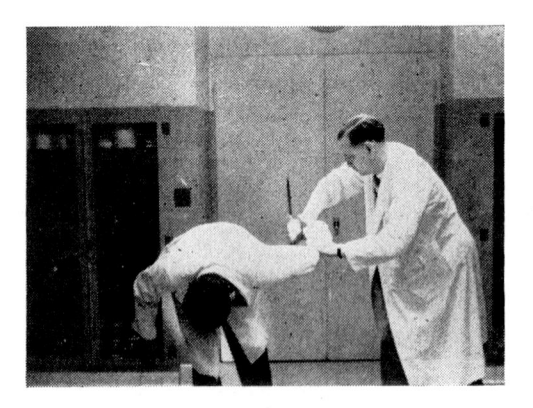

Fig. 165

With left hand *pull* the back of his left elbow down to your left and pull up with your right hand.

HOW TO USE A DAGGER

Fig. 166

Twist the dagger point down.

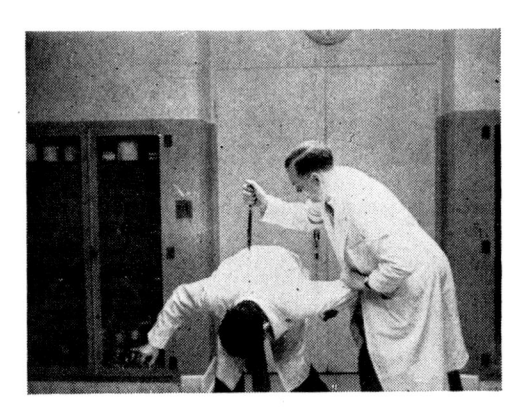

Fig. 167

Stab him in the back, pulling him to you with your left hand. Lean your weight onto the thrust.

ADDITIONAL NOTES FROM INSTRUCTOR ON CHAPTER 2.

Chapter 3

THE DAGGER OF THE ENEMY HOW TO AVOID IT.

In the following five movements your enemy holds a dagger in his right hand. You are unarmed.

No. 1
THE "TWO-HAND TWIST" DEFENCE-OFFENSE MOVEMENT AGAINST AN UPWARD THRUST

Remember—Speed is essential. Move faster than you have ever moved before. If anyone can see what's happening when you perform these movements, then you're doing them too slowly.

Practice slowly. The best incentive to make you practice *slowly* and *carefully* from the beginning, is to use a *sharp* knife. Of course when doing this you should be under the direct supervision of an instructor. No horseplay! This is serious.

To learn the essential movements practise these positions.

1.—Your opponent holds the dagger in his right hand with the blade pointing up.

2.—Reaching out quickly, the little finger edge of your right hand, palm down, *strikes* to your right against the outside of the blade close to his hand, pushing it over to your right (Fig. 168).

3.—Simultaneously your left hand, with palm up, scoops up against the base of the handle and against the under side of his hand, with the little finger edge of your left palm reaching up over his fingers.

Then with your left hand lever up and to your left as your right hand pushes the top of the dagger handle to your right.

This twists the knife blade down to your right between you and your opponent (Fig. 169).

4.—Twist it *right around*. With right hand pressure try to force the tip of the blade constantly up towards his right arm-pit bending his wrist. ***This is very important.*** You twist the dagger out of his grip *against his thumb*. Try to twist it right out of his hands into your hands, and stab him in the back. Left side spleen. Right side liver. Take your choice (Fig. 170).

* * *

Danger.—Do not cut your right hand on the edge of the knife. (Incidentally remember while doing this movement that he has a crotch and you have practised knee-blow calisthenics. Always crouch *low*. Bend forward.)

* * *

When is this defence movement most useful?
When you are wearing gloves, or mitts, in winter fighting. Practise with gloves on.

THE DAGGER OF THE ENEMY HOW TO AVOID IT

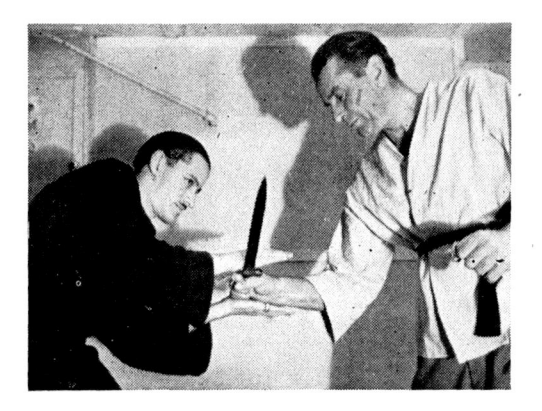

Fig. 168

Your right hand pushes to your right against the top of the dagger handle and your left hand pushes up to your left against the bottom of the dagger handle.

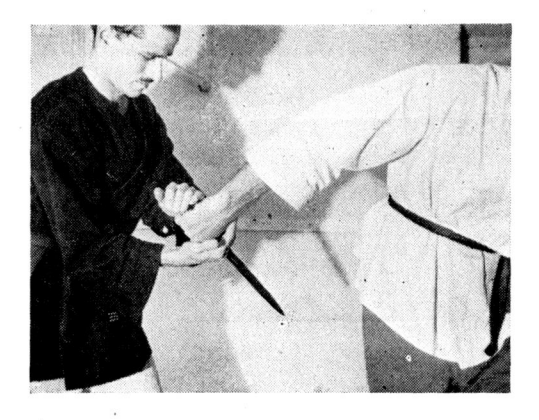

Fig. 169

Twist the blade down and around, keeping the tip of the blade pointing towards him and constantly forcing it up. Lever the dagger out of his grip.

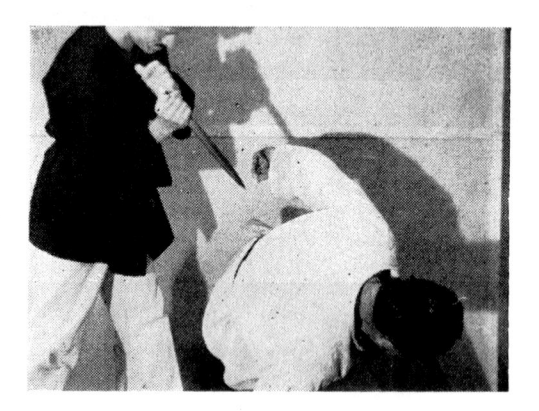

Fig. 170

Then with the dagger in both hands, stab down putting all your weight behind the thrust.

No. 2
THE LEFT HAND GRIP "ROLL" DEFENCE AGAINST AN UPWARD THRUST

How to flip a knife out of an opponent's hand.

Situation:

The enemy stabs *up* at you with the dagger held in his right hand, blade up.

What to do:

1.—Turn to your right out of the thrust, stepping back your right foot and crouching down, then grab *down* on his right wrist with your left hand. Your thumb points down, and your fingers go over the inside of his wrist (Fig. 171).

2.—With the little finger edge of your stiffened out right palm, which faces down, strike to your *right* against the top of the dagger handle which often projects a little above his fist. Strike to your right and down (Fig. 172).

3.—Now keeping the edge of your right hand pressing firmly against the dagger there, push it further down, levering it under his hand (Fig. 173).

4.—Then turning your palm down, bend his wrist in with the back of your right hand pressing against the dagger near the handle (Fig. 174).

5.—Slide your right hand onto the top of your left wrist, then push the back your right wrist forward, against the dagger (Fig. 175). Pry it out of his grip by levering your right wrist forward.

> This requires practice and experimentation. If you don't get it the first time, try again, trying to reason out any mistake. Try it several times, until you get the desired result.

190 ARWROLOGY

Danger: Unless you are wearing gloves you may cut yourself on the dagger. This defense movement is especially adaptable to winter fighting, when mitts are worn.

A Tip: Always attempt to lever the dagger handle *against* his thumb, and to bend in his wrist.

General Rule: When a wrist is bent in, the power to grasp anything is then reduced.

Professor C. P. Martin, of the Department of Anatomy at McGill University has shown that there is a perfectly logical anatomical explanation for this.

To prove this to yourself, bend in your right wrist as far as you can, so that it forms a right angle with your forearm. Then try to squeeze a cigarette package with your *finger tips, keeping your wrist bent in.*

You will find that your fingers have lost much of their gripping power. Then straighten your hand out and try again to crush the cigarette package with your *finger tips*. It is comparatively more easy now. (Have you taken the cigarettes out of the package?)

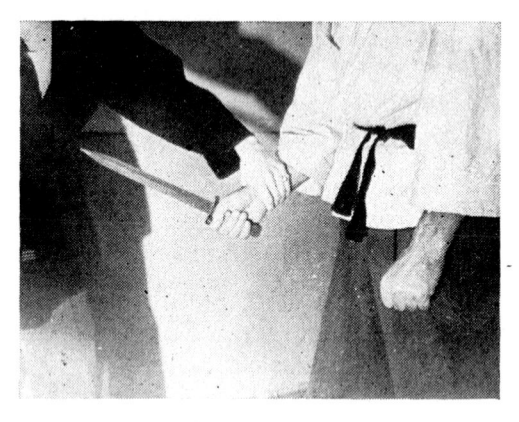

Fig. 171

Holding a dagger pointing upward in his right hand, your enemy has stabbed up at you. Fortunately you have managed to grab down on his right wrist with your left hand. How? Grabbing from his right side your left hand is turned so that your fingers go over the inside of his wrist, with your thumb against the outside of his wrist. Your thumb is the weak spot in your grip, so follow through quickly.

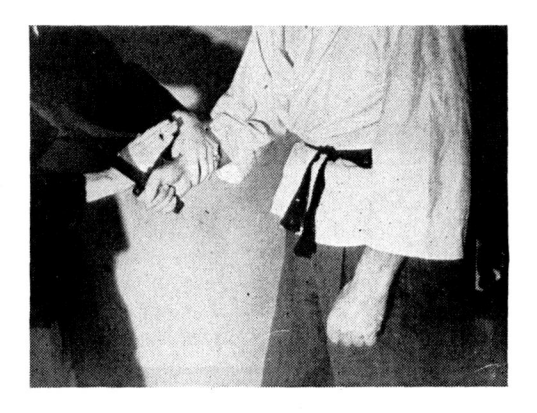

Fig. 172
Still holding his wrist with your left hand, so the blade of the knife points almost vertically upward, you strike against the top of the dagger handle at the base of the blade with the little finger edge of your right palm. Your palm faces down and you strike to your right. Your fingers are held out straight, tightly together.

192   ARWROLOGY

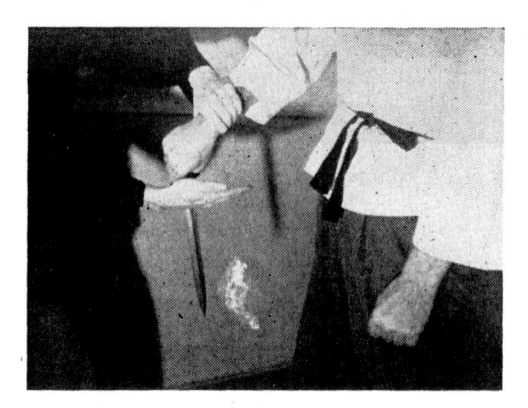

Fig. 173

Still holding his wrist with your left hand, after knocking the dagger to your right with the edge of your right hand, you lever it down *with the edge of your hand,* and push it under his wrist, around to your left. Your right palm now faces up.

(Your next movement in forcing the dagger to your left, is to turn your wrist so you right palm faces *down,* pushing the dagger to your left all the time.)

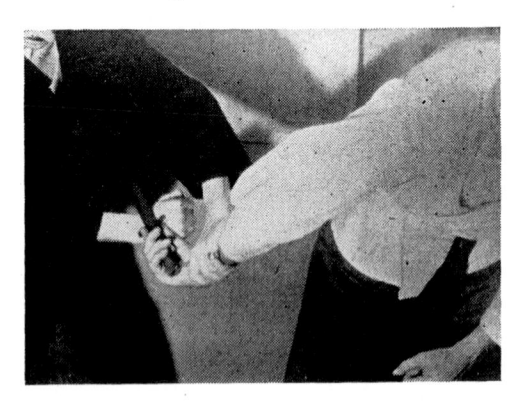

Fig. 174

After pushing the dagger to your left, lever it up *between your left arm and your body,* bending in his wrist to loosen his grip. You are pressing against the dagger now with the *back* of your right wrist.

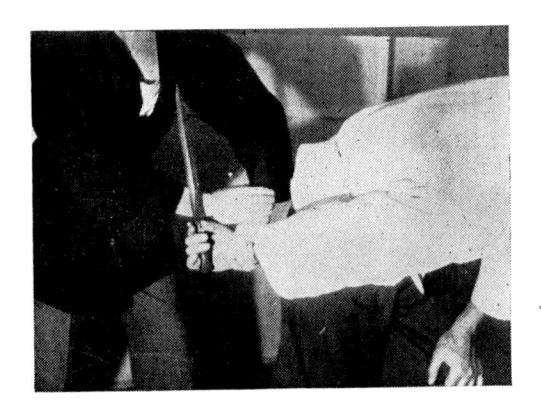

Fig. 175

Now slide your right hand onto the top of your left wrist, bringing your right elbow forward so the dagger is pressed forward by the angle between the back of your right hand and your right forearm.

Now with a forward flip of your right wrist you may lever the knife out of his hand.

Practise these movements until you get them accurately. Fit the positions in snugly.

HOW TO FLIP A CLUB OUT OF AN OPPONENT'S HAND

The methods of fighting illustrated in this book may be applied effectively to many circumstances other than those described. For instance the movements in the "Left Hand Grip 'Roll' Defence Against an Upward Thrust of a Dagger", just described, may be used to disarm a man who strikes down at you with a club.

Situation :

With a club in his right hand, your opponent strikes down at your head.

General Instructions :

1.—First, prevent being hit. Naturally. Crouch down, and grip his wrist with your left hand. Keep your right wrist crossed in front of your face immediately behind your left wrist as a secondary defence against the blow (Fig. 176). Your right hand is kept in position for edge-hand blows, with fingers out straight and close together.

2.—Still holding his right wrist in your left hand, push the club down to your right by forcing against the club just above his grip with the little finger edge of your right hand, palm facing down (Fig. 177).

HOW TO FLIP A CLUB OUT OF AN OPPONENT'S HAND

Fig. 176

He strikes down at your head. Cross your right hand behind your left wrist. Grab his wrist with your left hand, and at the same time strike up against his wrist near his hand with the little finger edge of your right wrist or stiffened out hand.

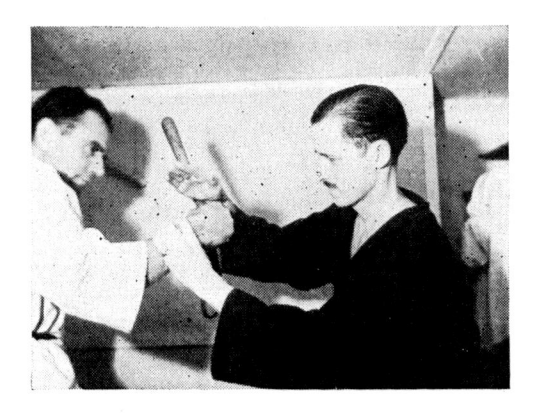

Fig. 177

Keeping your right hand out stiff, slip it over his fist against the club just above his grip. Push the club to your right and down with the little finger edge of your right hand.

3.—Push the club down then swing it around and up to your left by pushing it with your right wrist. If he still hangs on to the club, his wrist will be twisted around into such a position that a firm grip is difficult for him to maintain (Fig. 178).

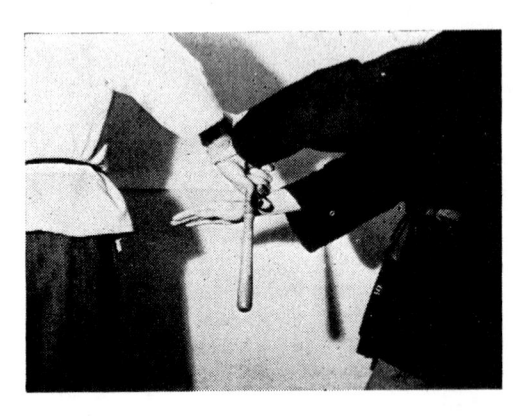

Fig. 178

After pushing the club down past a horizontal position, keep your right palm facing down by turning your hand around, and push the club to your left with the *thumb edge* of your right *wrist*.

4.—Lower your left elbow and slide your right hand on top of your left wrist, up close to the club handle.

Then force your right wrist forward, levering the club out of his grip as his wrist is bent. To gain leverage, press your fingers against your left wrist as you raise your right wrist forward against the club (Fig. 179).

Remember to employ "Blow Power" in all these methods, before and after you have obtained your objective.

HOW TO FLIP A CLUB OUT OF AN OPPONENT'S HAND

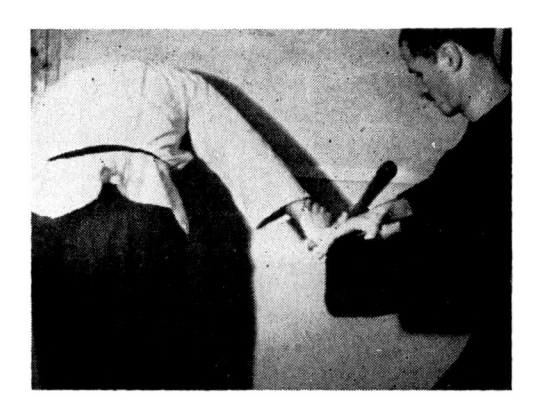

Fig. 179

Lowering your left elbow, reach the fingers of your right hand on to the TOP of your left wrist under the club. Keep your right wrist pressing against the club *close to his* fist.

Then a forward flip of your right wrist against the club will *bend his wrist in* and lever the club out of his grasp.

> Keep your left hand grip firmly on his right wrist throughout these movements.
> Your opponent may turn to his right with you. Watch out for this!
> The fundamental point here is turning his wrist around and bending it in on itself, so his hand looses its gripping power.

No. 3

ARM-LOCK DEFENCE AGAINST AN UPWARD THRUST

Situation :

Your enemy holds a dagger in his right hand with the blade pointing up and he stabs up at you.

Criticism :

More likely he would *weave* the dagger about so you would not know when or where he's going to stab you. That is true enough. When your enemy holds a dagger in his hand and you're unarmed, the odds *are* against you. But if you have practised some definite movements of defence then you will have a better chance of defeating him. The more methods you know, the better your chance, and the less you have to rely on luck.

What may you do?

1.—With your left wrist, thumb down and the palm of your left hand turned towards him, knock his wrist to your right and a little up. Turn right as you do this (Fig. 180).

Why turn right?

(1) To get out of way of the dagger.
(2) To give power to your left hand blow.
You turn right for only a "fraction" of a second, then swing around to your left as,

2.—Your left forearm pushes his right wrist further up and towards him, probably bending his elbow.

3.—Your right FOREARM goes *over* his right forearm, your right elbow bend clamping his wrist tightly, then slide your right WRIST *under* your left forearm and your right HAND goes *over* your left upper arm just above your left elbow (Fig. 181).

THE DAGGER OF THE ENEMY HOW TO AVOID IT

Tip :
Clamp in tightly to get this. In early practice bring your elbows close together after you have applied the lock. Then to increase pressure about his wrist pull your elbows away from each other. Keep your palms down and the little finger edge of your hands facing forwards and slightly up.

4.—Lever the knife away. Force your left wrist forward against his right wrist. Pull his elbow into you snugly, by tugging down and into your stomach with your right arm, which clamps the upper limit of his forearm near his elbow.

Your right forearm in its turn may be forced down against his right shoulder and chest as you lever his forearm back.

5.—You may put your right leg behind him in an attempt to trip him backwards, or instead you may lever him down by leaning forward and stepping back with your right foot and going down on your right knee, applying pressure on his arm with your lock.

At anytime be ready to deliver a right edge-hand blow to the right side of his neck.

ADVICE : Watch his left fist.

Keep the fingers, wrist and forearm of your right arm straight, stiffened out like a plank. On occasion you may slip your right hand out and give him an edge-hand blow with your right hand against the right side of his neck. Remember crotch blows with your knees.

In the mastering of all these methods there is an important fact to realize:

Instructions followed rigidly, may work one hundred percent against one man of a certain height, strength and weight, but they will not work so well against another man of a different physique.

The "Art" of Arwrology involves to a great extent the ability to modify each and every method to the various types of opponents.

In time, you will acquire little tricks of your own which will help YOU to smooth out your difficulties and to overcome your enemies.

Fig. 180

He thrusts up. Your left hand swoops around and knocks his wrist away to your right. Note that you strike with the little finger edge of your left hand and wrist.

> Observe the defender's lythe, powerful position—shortened neck, tight stiffened fingers, lowered right shoulder. That's technique.

THE DAGGER OF THE ENEMY HOW TO AVOID IT

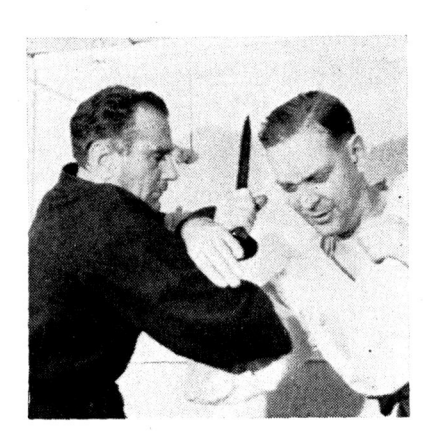

Fig. 181

With your left hand you have forced his right hand back. Your right arm has gone around his forearm over his bent elbow, then UNDER YOUR LEFT wrist. Then your right hand goes on TOP of your left upper arm. Clamp snugly. Keep his forearm VERTICAL. Lever his hand away and his elbow into you.

> (You may lever him over backwards, pressing your right elbow AGAINST his right shoulder. When he's down don't forget a foot on the knife, and kicks.)

No. 4

"ARM ABOUT TWIST" DEFENCE AGAINST A DOWNWARD THRUST

Situation : Your enemy holds a dagger in his right hand, with the blade pointing *down,* and he wildly stabs down at you.

What to do :

1.—Crouch low (Fig. 182).

2.—With the palm of your right hand facing forward, grab up at his right wrist.

3.—Then pull his arm around to your right, pushing the back of his right elbow with your left hand (Fig. 183).

4.—Pull his right wrist to your right hip,—keeping the dagger pointing away from you all the time, naturally. Turn a little to your right.

5.—Lever him down pushing the BACK of his right elbow forward and pulling back on his right wrist (Figs. 184 and 185). Your left leg put across the front of his legs will help to trip him forward.

6.—When he's down, lever the knife out of his hand, stepping on the knife or on his hand if necessary.

And remember the rule: "When he's down, follow up."
Don't just think that because he's down, he's overcome.

Tip: When learning this method, have your opponent stab down at you repeatedly with some harmless object, so that you may develop good eye and muscle co-ordination.

Occasionally have your partner pick up your left leg with his left hand, during this defence when you place your left leg across the front of his legs. Practise immediately giving a left edge-hand blow against the right side of his neck or against his ribs as soon as he pulls up your leg.

THE DAGGER OF THE ENEMY HOW TO AVOID IT

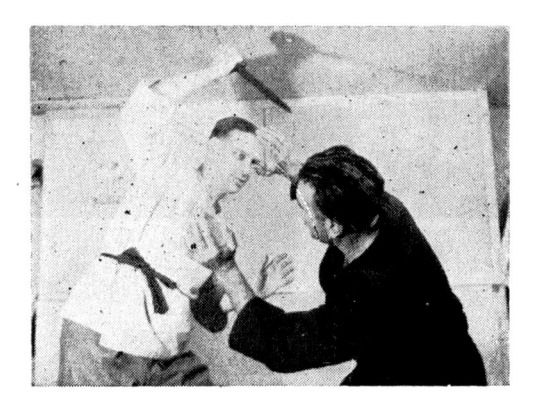

Fig. 182

Wildly he stabs down at you. Keep low.

Fig. 183

Your right hand, with palm facing forward, grabs up at his right wrist with your thumb going *under* his wrist and your fingers going over the top of his wrist. Your left hand, fingers pointing upward, pushes the back of his right elbow up to your right.

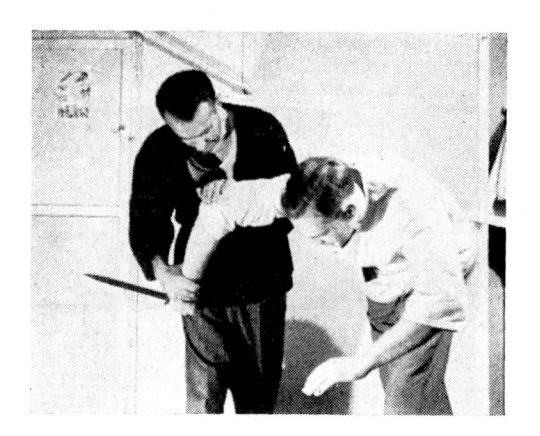

Fig. 184

Pull his right wrist down and around, holding it tightly to your right side. Your left hand pushes his elbow forward.—Then put your left leg across the front of his legs.

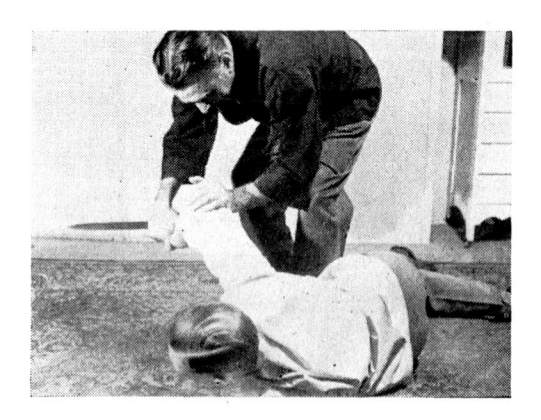

Fig. 185

Lever him down. Then disarm him and follow up.

No. 5

ARM-LOCK DEFENCE AGAINST A DOWNWARD JAB.

In the last defence against a downward thrust, we assumed that you could *grab* your opponent's wrist. But that is not always easily done.

Think back. What method already described, with which you do not have to grab his wrist, could be used against a downward stab?

You may use the principle of "No. 3, Arm-Lock Defence Against An Upward Thrust." (Figs. 180, 181).

When your opponent stabs down at you with a dagger held pointing down in his right hand, with your *left* wrist knock his right wrist up. Loop your right arm over his right forearm and slide your right hand under your left forearm onto the top of your left upper arm. Clamp his arm tightly (Fig. 186). Then follow through as already described.

Give him blows with your knees. Guard your head and body with your right elbow against a left hand blow. Bring him to the ground.

Fig. 186

You have guarded against a downward stab by knocking his right wrist up with your left wrist. Then looping your right arm over his arm, slide your right hand under your left forearm on to the top of your left upper arm. Clamp his arm tightly.

Lever him back. Get the dagger. Then get him.

* * *

There are various other arm-locks which may be used here in certain circumstances, but they are relatively less efficient.

One is very similar to this lock except that instead of knocking his right wrist up with your *left* wrist, you knock it up with your *right* wrist.

Instructions: As he stabs down at you with the dagger held in his right hand, knock up his right wrist with your *right* wrist, at the same time sliding your left arm over his right arm. Then slip your left hand down between his wrist and your right wrist, going under your right wrist to press against the thumb edge of your right wrist. Force his arm back.

If you can follow that you'd make a good mathematician, and Arwrologist too!

* * *

Another hold is a two hand grip on his wrist with one thumb crossing over the other. Painful crushing pressure may sometimes be exerted over the bones of his wrist by this method.

Beware of his other arm.

What Next?

These are just a few of the more simple methods which may be of use when either you or your opponent has a dagger. There are other, more dramatic methods. These are described in another volume.

They include such tricks as defending yourself against a right hand *upward* stab by grabbing down on his right wrist with both hands, with your thumbs crossing over the thumb edge of his wrist, and your fingers, which point towards his fingers, clasping under his wrist.

Then swinging your left elbow and arm over his right arm and tugging his arm down and away from his body, duck your left shoulder and head under his right arm-pit. Then heave him back over your right shoulder so that the dagger, still in his hand, can be twisted towards him and forcefully driven into his stomach as you throw him over your head.

* * *

Remember that a man fighting for his life nearly always pulls in his arm tightly to his body whenever his wrist is grasped. Unless you are fast and thorough, and direct his attention elsewhere by kicks and knee blows, many problems may arise. It is always wise to direct your opponent's attention away from the part of his body which you intend to attack.

When both you and your enemy are armed with a dagger, other special methods are applicable and these will be described in future volumes on Arwrology.

ADDITIONAL NOTES FROM INSTRUCTOR ON CHAPTER 3.

Chapter 4

BAYONET THRUST DEFENCE-OFFENSE MOVEMENT.

When describing fighting methods with a dagger or a bayonet used as a dagger, it is worth while mentioning at least one defence-offense movement for an unarmed man against an enemy armed with rifle and bayonet.

A dagger has a handle which may be used to deliver back-hand blows, and a rifle with bayonet has a steel capped butt which may be used to deliver blows with.

Be prepared for either end of a dagger or a rifle with bayonet. The following method is described so as to give the unarmed man something to practise so that he will know what it *feels* like to be against a man armed with rifle and bayonet, and to eliminate some of the surprise element. It is an example of one of the many methods which an unarmed soldier may attempt in defending himself against a bayonet thrust. Actually the odds are against you. Kicks, knee blows and edge-hand blows should always be used.

Problem Facing You :

One of the enemy runs at you with his rifle gripped tightly in his hands and his bayonet going straight for your chest.

You are standing unarmed in front of him.

General Directions :

1.—First push *yourself* away from the rifle. Do not try to push the rifle away. There is a difference. Assume that he is much stronger than you are.

As he thrusts forward at your chest, strike against the rifle barrel just a little further toward the muzzle than his left hand grip. The blow is given with the little finger edge of your left hand, your hand pointing *down*, your wrist turned so that your palm, open, faces him. Your fingers and thumb are held tightly together, out stiff. At the same time, straighten out your left arm, pushing yourself away from the rifle.

Swerve back to your right, with your right foot going back, thus facing him sideways, on his right side. You have now pushed yourself away from the rifle. This is a most important point, because if you do not push yourself out of line of the bayonet thrust in time, knowledge of many holds will not be of much use.

2.—Now grasp the rifle barrel with your left hand. How? After hitting the barrel to your right with the little finger edge of your open left hand, which points down, twist your palm around so it faces forward then your thumb which points down, can slip over the top of the barrel. Grip the barrel tightly, your fingers curling under the right side of the barrel.

Pull the bayonet end of the rifle up over to your left, between you and your enemy. Slide your right hand, palm up and open, under your left arm in order to grab the other end of the rifle, just a little above his right hand grip (Fig. 187).

3.—Your right hand is held palm up as though you were a waiter balancing a tray. Hook the rifle in the angle between your thumb and fingers. Your fingers are held tightly together. Push the butt end of the rifle down to your right between you and your enemy. Lever the butt of the rifle down and to your right with your right hand grip, keeping your right elbow in tightly to your right side to contribute firmness. At the same moment with your left hand grip on the rifle barrel you pull it up and to your left. Get in close to him, leading with a powerful right knee blow into his crotch (Figs. 188 and 191). (Remember the Knee Blow Psycho-Physical Calisthenics?)

4.—Then twist the muzzle of the gun **DOWN** to your left and flip **UP** the butt trying to strike the left side of his head with the butt, thus tearing the rifle out of his grasp (Fig. 189).

5.—Still keeping your same grip on the rifle, swing the butt across the front of your face to your left so the butt lies on top of your left shoulder.

Here your right arm is across the front of your chest above your left arm. Your right hand grips downward on the rifle, butt end, and your left hand grips upward on the rifle, bayonet end. Aim the bayonet at your enemy (Fig. 190).

From this position you can heave the rifle a javelin, or thrust forward, or swing the butt down or around like a club.

Fig. 187

Suppose your opponent on the left has made a forward lunge at you with the bayonet on his rifle.

Guard against the bayonet by striking the end of the rifle with the little finger edge of your left hand, *palm facing him,* and jump to his right. Then, as shown above, grasp the end of the rifle a little up from his left hand, with your thumb looping over the barrel and your fingers grabbing under the right side of the upper end of the rifle.

Slip your right hand under your left with palm up to grab the rifle just above his right hand grip, as your left hand pulls the upper end of his rifle over to your left.

BAYONET THRUST DEFENCE-OFFENSE MOVEMENT

Fig. 188

Your right hand, *palm up,* fingers stiffly together and thumb out, grabs the rifle in the angle between your fingers and thumb just above his right hand grip and pulls it up to your right.

With left hand swing the bayonet end of the rifle up over to your left, and with your right hand, which now grabs up on the rifle more firmly, push the butt end further up to your right.

Give a hard right knee blow to his crotch while you are twisting the rifle around.

(Remember the rule : "When he grabs with both hands, Strike!" Here he's grabbing his rifle with both hands. So give a powerful high knee blow to his crotch to induce him to loosen his grip on the rifle.)

Fig. 189

Swing the butt of the rifle up against the right side of his face and pull the bayonet end down to your left. Make that knee blow count.

Fig. 190

Keep your same grip on the rifle and swing the butt end on your left shoulder. The bayonet end is aimed at your opponent.

BAYONET THRUST DEFENCE—OFFENSE MOVEMENT

Criticism : Too complicated. Practically have to be an expert to rely on it.

Other methods : Naturally in order to cope with attack from various angles, you should practice many other methods for defence against a rifle with bayonet assault. Most of these methods suggest grabbing the rifle near the bayonet with one hand and near the butt with the other, and twisting the rifle around out of your opponent's grip. Occasionally you can put a leg behind your opponent and trip him back over it, or grabbing the rifle and ducking down low and turning your back to him you can throw him over your head, "flying mare" style.

A Simple and Effective Method.

As your opponent thrusts forward, with your left hand push the bayonet end of the rifle to your right, grabbing it tightly.

Then swing your right arm over the barrel end of the gun, clamping it tightly in your right arm-pit, and slide your right hand under the rifle, gripping it tightly near the middle.

Pull the rifle and your opponent to you and give a back edge-hand blow at his neck with your left hand, and give knee-to-crotch blows. (A Step Back Trip Throw may be used here sometimes.)

Fig. 191

The knee blow to his crotch is very important. It generally induces him to slacken his grip on the rifle.

ADDITIONAL NOTES FROM INSTRUCTOR ON CHAPTER 4.

PART V

Chapter I

STRANGLE HOLD DEFENCE

This whole procedure is primarily one of escape.

Situation:

A powerful man tries to strangle you with his hands (Fig. 192).

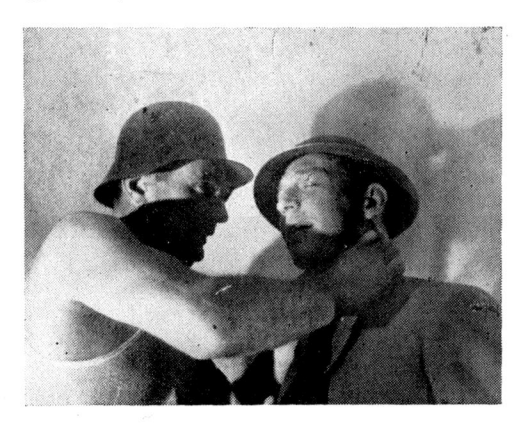

Fig. 192
He's got you by the throat.

You've got about five seconds. Your main objective is to get his hands off your neck. Do this.

Instructions:

1.—Shorten your neck by hunching up your shoulders. Slip your right hand UNDER his left arm and grab his right wrist (Fig. 193).

Fig. 193

Hunch up your shoulders and pull down on his left wrist with your right hand.

2.—Swing your left arm and elbow *over* his right wrist and slide your left hand *under* his left wrist (Fig. 194).

> *Important Point*: You may swing your left elbow far to your right, over his right forearm, between you and your opponent, and *clamp* his right wrist firmly to you by clamping your left upper arm tightly to your chest and leaning forward.
>
> This is a great help often in pulling his right hand down from your throat. Your right hand pulls his right wrist down at the same time.
>
> When you have loosened his right hand grip on your neck, slide your left hand under his left wrist. Your thumb should be pointing down with your palm facing forward.

STRANGLE HOLD DEFENCE

Fig. 194

Passing your left arm over his right forearm clamp it to you and at the same time your right hand pulls his right wrist down sharply. Then your left hand, fingers out stiff and palm forward, slides UNDER his left wrist.

Then with the little finger edge of your left hand near your wrist, push up against the under part of his left wrist (Figs. 194 and 199).

3.—You may pull back to your right to help release his left hand grip. As soon as it is loosened from your neck, grab *up* at his left wrist with your left hand, thumb down, palm facing forward (Figs. 199 and 200).

Make the pushing up and then the grabbing of his left wrist one continuous motion. Pull his left hand over and down to your left, and at the same time pull his right wrist under his left arm (Fig. 195).

Then if lucky you may powerfully jerk his left arm out straight and down with your left hand grip, and force his right arm over the back of his left arm. Hold his right arm firmly over the back of his left elbow

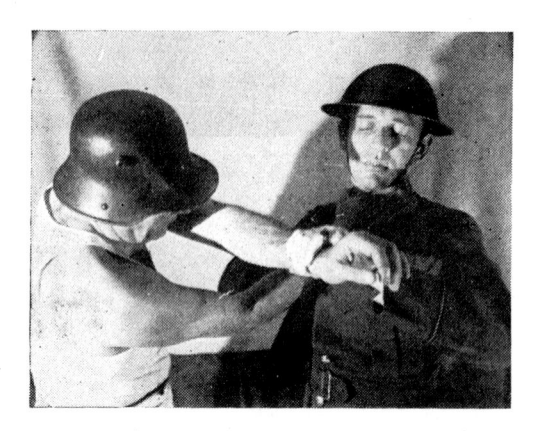

Fig. 195

With your left hand lever his left arm up and pull it over to your left. With your right hand yank his right wrist down and to your left.

Now your immediate objective has been accomplished. His hands are off your throat.

(Fig. 200). Then pull up suddenly on his left wrist with your left hand in an attempt to injure his left elbow joint. Facing him, give him a right knee blow to his crotch (Fig. 196). You may put your right leg past the outside and *behind* his right leg and throw him back over it, turning a little to your left.

Criticism : It is almost impossible to pull a fighting man's arm out straight.

Comment : The main point is to get his hands off your throat, and fast. What you do after that depends on the circumstance.

At any time you can bring up your right knee to his crotch.

Further Criticism : What about the rule,

"When he grabs you with both hands, STRIKE!"

Comment : When your enemy grabs you about the throat with both hands, you may be able to smash at his head and neck with back edge-hand blows, and you

STRANGLE HOLD DEFENCE

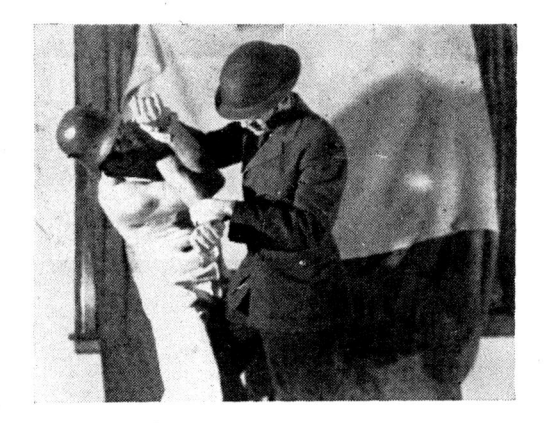

Fig. 196

You may be able to pull down his left arm and loop his right arm up over the back of his left elbow and pull sharply back on his left wrist in an effort to incapacitate his left elbow. Bring your right knee up into his crotch or put your right leg behind him and throw him over it.

---

certainly should make good use of your feet and knees. Stamp your heels on his toes. Kick him in the shin. Deliver knee blows to his crotch and stomach. Kick the side and back of his legs with your heels—right foot kicking right leg.

But what takes precedence here over everything else is to get his hands immediately off your throat.

Any Complications? Yes. Your opponent may press his head in close to you making it difficult to hit. And besides that, the Nazi have been taught some elementary Judo and some Japanese are supposed to be "Experts" in Judo, Jiu-Jitsu, Tan-Jitsu and Taku-Jitsu. So watch your opponent's feet. He may try to trip you off balance or give you knee blows.

If you are thrown to the ground the counter movement against the strangle hold does not vary (Figs. 197 and 198).

"TIPS" ON STRANGLE HOLD DEFENCE

Fig. 197

If your opponent (man in white jacket) leaps at you, pushing you to the ground, and pinning you there, tries to choke you, just follow the same procedure already described.—

1.—Your right arm goes UNDER his left arm and grabs his right wrist.

2.—Your left arm goes OVER his right arm and UNDER his left wrist. (Remember 1. Right under; 2. Left over.)

STRANGLE HOLD DEFENCE

Fig. 198

After twisting your body to your left and levering out of his grip by pulling down his right wrist and flipping up his left wrist, hang on to his wrists and secure this lock, throwing him over on his back with you at his right side.

Criticism : MAYBE you can injure his left elbow by pulling his left wrist up and forcing down on his right wrist, so his right arm acts as a fulcrum against his left arm, the lever. But that's not enough.
You must "Follow Up." That's a rule. Remember he's still conscious, so think about blows, kicks and Arwr locks!

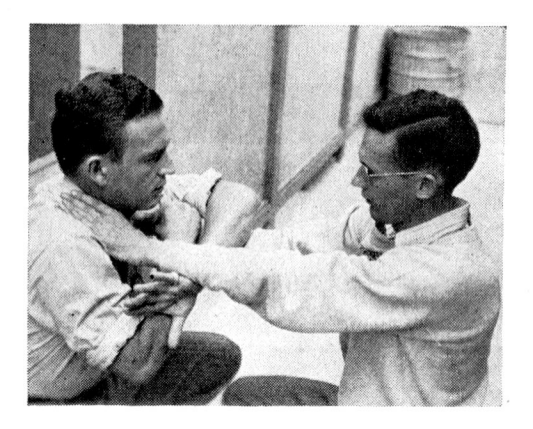

Fig. 199

Note that your left wrist, at the base of your little finger, with palm forward, is ready to push up his left wrist.

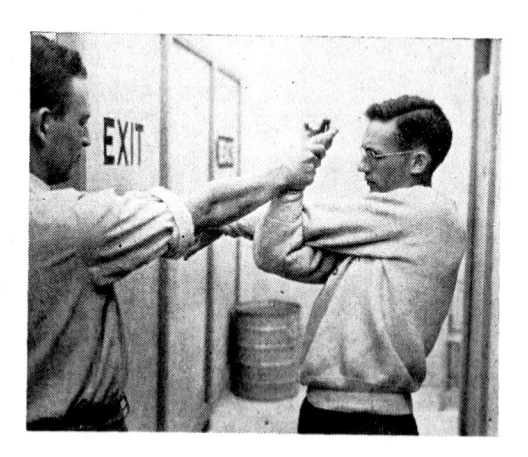

Fig. 200

Note that your left hand, after pushing his left wrist up, GRABS his left wrist, pulls it to your left, while your right hand raises his right arm over the back of his right elbow. Then you push with your right hand and pull with your left hand. This is the beginning of his exit.

STRANGLE HOLD DEFENCE

Some methods hardly worth mentioning :

When a man grabs you by the throat, there are several defence methods which you may try, such as jabbing your fingers into his eyes, into the parotid gland below and behind his ear, into the submaxillary gland under his jaw; grabbing hair, tearing down his lower lip with your nails, pulling and twisting or hitting his ears with open cupped palms; also the method of clasping your hands together and thrusting them up between his arms and striking back and forth, also passing one arm up between his arms and pushing him in the face, or reaching over his arms with one hand and striking or pushing him back with the edge of your hand under his nose, or striking just above the bridge of his nose (Glabella), or twisting his head around, or kicking him; also there is the method of slipping your left hand up between his arms and over his right arm, clamping it to your left side, and pushing his left elbow up and over to your left and tripping him back over your right leg which you place behind his right leg. These methods may work *IF* your opponent tries to choke you *with his arms far outstretched.*—A ridiculous situation. A man strangling you comes in close.

But there is one frequently helpful thing to remember in doing the defence "Escape" movement recommended, and that is this:—

After you have levered his hands off your throat, you may give him a hard edge-hand blow with your right hand against the carotid sinus in the right side of his neck. This *has* knocked men out.

SUMMARY :

If he grabs your throat with both hands,

1.—Grab his right wrist with your right hand *going under his left arm.*
2.—Grab his left wrist with your left hand *going over his right arm.*
3.—Pull his right wrist down to your right.
4.—Push his left wrist up to your left.
5.—Cross his arms and throw him over your right leg.

Adaptation to Military Psycho-Physical Calisthenics :

Have one man, standing still, try the defence against ten to a hundred men moving past him in single file, each one stopping in front of him and grabbing him by the throat. Each man in the group should have an opportunity to test out the defence movement.

ADDITIONAL NOTES FROM INSTRUCTOR
ON CHAPTER 1.

Chapter 2

THE ANKLE CLAMP THROWS

1.—Face Forward   (a) From his left side
                         (b) From his right side
2.—Head Back   (a) From his left side
                         (b) From his right side

A word of caution

The first time you try these throws, be sure your partner has someone to catch him as he falls.

1.—(a) Face Forward, From his LEFT side (Fig. 201).

Here you spring down at your opponent from his *left* side and a little behind him, and place your left knee *on* the ground across the front of his left foot. Then you pass behind him putting your right foot firmly on the ground behind him.

Rest your right elbow momentarily on top of your right knee, which you keep upright and OFF THE GROUND. Then pass your left arm around the outside of his *right* ankle and bring your left wrist across the *front* of his ankle. Then slip your right hand between his ankles, from behind, grabbing your left wrist. Pull his ankles together and heave forward pulling his ankles back, throwing him on his face.

> IF he sits down on you, because you were too slow and did not put enough forward pushing power into your attack, rest your right elbow on your right knee to give support, and heave him over backwards.

228 ARWROLOGY

**Face Forward
From His LEFT Side**

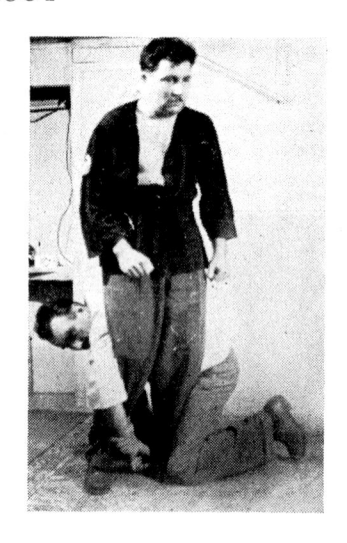

Fig. 201

Approaching your opponent from his left side, kneel down on your left knee, placing it across the *front* of his left foot.

Then passing *behind* him, bending your right knee but NOT putting it down on the ground, bring your left arm around the outside of his right leg and across the FRONT of his right ankle.

Then pass your right hand between his ankles from behind and grab your left wrist.

Throw him flat on his face by pulling his ankles together, then back, and heaving him forward with your body. Yank his ankles back, up high.

Caution: Watch his right hand, as he may try to grab a handfull of hair, or deliver a back-hand blow at your face.

* * *

1.—(b) **Face Forward, From his RIGHT side.**
(Figs. 202, 203, 204, 205).

Here the mechanism is the same, only you attack him from his *right* side, so put your right knee down across the *front* of his right foot. Pass behind him.

Bring your right arm around the front of his left ankle. Slip your left hand between his ankles and grab your right wrist. Pull his ankles together and then yank them back and heave him forward onto his face.

> Immediately follow up the advantage of having thrown your opponent on his face. Hobble up towards his head, holding him down flat with a hand in the centre of his back. Deliver knee blows to ribs, back edge-hand blows to the sides and back of his neck. Even back heel-kicks to the temple, neck or ribs may be used if you can get into the proper position to deliver them. (Review Part I, Chapter 4, How To Kick The Enemy When He Is Down.)
>
> If you have to keep low perhaps out of line of fire, get a Posterior Arwr Lock on his neck as soon as possible. (Review Part II, Chapter 4.)
>
> If you have a knife, remember the spleen is on the left side of his back behind the ninth, tenth, and eleventh ribs, (the lower ribs), and his vocal cords are in front of the neck. Cut below his 'Adam's Apple' to silence him.
>
> The Ankle Clamp Throws are designed so that your opponent will probably break his own wrists in his fall. Be careful when practising these throws. Before letting yourself be thrown, be sure you know how to fall without injury, or have someone to catch you as you fall.

From His RIGHT Side

Face Forward

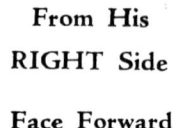

Fig. 202

Here you attack your opponent from his *right* side, kneeling your right knee down across the front of his right foot, then passing *behind* him you reach your right arm out around the outside of his left leg and across the front of his left ankle.

Then pass your left hand between his ankles and grab your right wrist.

Your left foot is on the ground behind him and your left knee is OFF the ground. Your left leg gives you forward pushing power when you throw him forward on his face.

How? By pulling his ankles together, jerking his left ankle back, and heaving him forward with the right side of your body.

> Your right knee across the front of his right foot prevents him from stepping forward to prevent the fall.
>
> This throw must be executed fast, or he may try to stab you in the back if he has a dagger, as the Major points out in the Illustration.

THE ANKLE CLAMP THROWS

**From His
RIGHT Side**

Face Forward

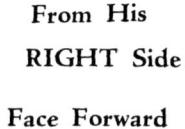

Fig. 203

What's wrong here? You have both knees ON THE GROUND. Your left knee should be OFF the ground to give you better balance, more forward pushing power and to enable you to rise to your feet quickly. Your left foot should be on the ground behind your opponent, and your left knee bent, but off the ground.

> You see, here your opponent may sit down on you with good effect. The farther apart your opponent's legs are separated, the harder it is to do the throw. And be careful not to get his left heel in your mouth when you pull his left leg back to throw him forward.

Face Forward
From His RIGHT Side

Fig. 204

*How To Practice The Throw—
Psycho-Physical Calisthenics*

Have two men face each other, standing about four or five feet apart. One man is to be thrown, and the other is to catch him as he falls.

Then like a black bat swoop down at the feet of the man on your left. Crouch behind him putting your right knee down across the *front* of his right foot. Your left foot is on the ground behind him and your left knee is bent but *off* the floor.

Pass your right arm around the outside of his left ankle, then bring your right hand across the front of his left ankle and then between his ankles. Then from behind grab your right wrist with your left hand between his ankles. Now you are ready to throw him face forward.

THE ANKLE CLAMP THROWS

Face Forward
From His RIGHT Side

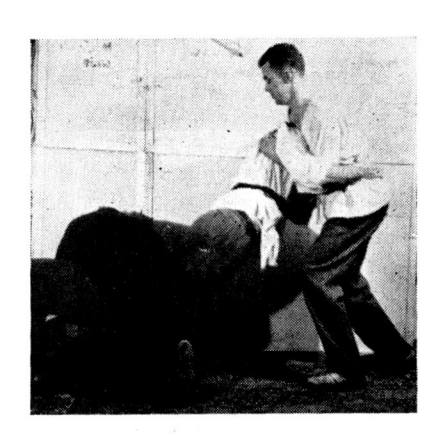

Fig. 205

Throw him on his face by pulling his ankles together then powerfully back and up. At first he is to fall into the arms of the man facing him.

When he *really* knows how to fall without injury he is to fall directly to the ground.

※　※　※

2.—(a) Head Back, From his LEFT side.

In this variation of the Ankle Clamp Throw, you approach your opponent's *left* side then kneel your right knee down *behind* his left foot, and passing in *front* of him, pass your right arm across the front of his ankles, around the outside of his right ankle, then behind it. Pass your left hand between his ankles from the front and grab your right wrist. Your left foot is planted firmly on the ground in *front* of him and your left knee is off the ground and up vertically. You may rest your left elbow on your left knee. Jerk his ankles together. Then pull them forward and up and at the same time heave him back with your right shoulder.

This has to be done fast as you are open to attack by his arms and his fists. As you throw him, avoid a kick in the face.

2.—(b) Head Back; From his RIGHT side.

Here you approach his right side. Kneel your left knee *behind* his right foot. Rest your right foot in front of him, with the knee off the ground and upright. Pass in front of him and reach your left arm across the front of his ankles, around the outside of his left ankle and behind it. Then pass your right hand between his ankles from in front and grab your left wrist. Clamp his ankles together and jerk them up forward as you heave him back with your left shoulder (Fig. 206).

Incidentally, in the *"Head Back"* throws, if you spend too much time trying to get the hold, and your opponent manages to grab you by the hair or neck, immediately forget about the throw and drive an elbow up into his crotch or stomach.

In any method, if resistance appears imminent, give blows in preference to getting holds. That is a general rule. Whatever you can do faster, do it!

After throwing an opponent backwards, remember to follow up with the fast exactitude of a veteran bill collector, but use blows, kicks and Arwr locks.

Head Back   **From His RIGHT Side**

Fig. 206

Kneel your left knee on the ground snugly *behind* his right leg, and well to the left of his right foot.

Stretch your left arm and body across the front of his legs and wind your left arm *behind* his left ankle.

Pass your right hand between his legs from in front and grab your left wrist. Heave him over backwards.

ANKLE CLAMP THROW
PSYCHO-PHYSICAL CALISTHENICS
FOR THE ARMED FORCES

Form two lines of ten to a hundred men, two paces apart, facing each other at a distance of about two paces. The men on the left are the "Falling Men". They will be thrown. Those on the right are the "Catching Men". They will catch the men facing them, who are to be thrown face forward, one after the other, by the student.

Now the student who is to practise the throw approaches the first of the "Falling Men" and throws him forward into the waiting arms of the first of the "Catching Men". Then the student approaches the next "Falling Man" in the line and throws him into the waiting arms of the "Catching Man" facing him. The student then attacks the next "Falling Man", and the next, and the next, throwing them all in quick succession. When he has thrown all the men in that line, he can start coming down the other line. In this case the "Catching Men" become "Falling Men", and vice versa.

This *"One Against Many"* training routine is to develop

1.—SPEED. Time the student and see how long it takes him to throw ten to a hundred men, one after another.

2.—TECHNIQUE. There are individual differences physically and psychologically in different opponents and only a varied experience in throwing men of different size and proportions will help to develop technique in applying the throw.

3.—RELAXATION. There is an element of play in group exercises of this nature which is very important psychologically.

Each man should have an opportunity of throwing the group. All the variations of the throw may be rehearsed in this manner (Fig. 207).

Psycho-Physical Calisthenics For The Ankle Clamp Throw, Face Forward, From His Right Side

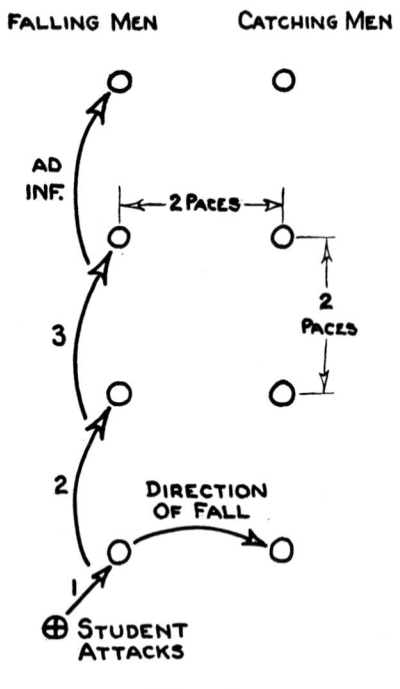

Fig. 207

Practice Routine To Develop Speed, Stamina and Adaptability.

ADDITIONAL NOTES FROM INSTRUCTOR ON CHAPTER 2.

Chapter 3

DEFENCE-OFFENSE MOVEMENTS AGAINST A GRIP ON YOUR WRIST

Situation :

Facing you, your opponent grabs *down* on your right wrist with his right hand. His thumb goes over the outside of your wrist and his fingers curl over the inside of your wrist. Got it? (Fig. 208, No. 1).

What to do :

1.—Swing your hand to your left, forcing your wrist against his *fingers* (Fig. 209 and Fig. 208, No. 2). If he resists, all the better.

2.—Then swing your hand up to your right (Fig. 210 and Fig. 208, No. 3).

3.—Then lever your fist over the top of his wrist to your left (Fig. 208, No. 4), and down, against his thumb, getting out of the grip (Fig. 208, No. 5).

4.—Then strike against the right side of his neck with the little finger edge of your stiff right hand (Fig. 211).

> Then you may immediately apply one of the most deadly of all holds the Anterior Arwr Lock. (Described in Volume II). When you hit a man with the back of your elbow or the edge of your hand you may often follow up with a knee blow to the crotch then a toe kick to his shin.

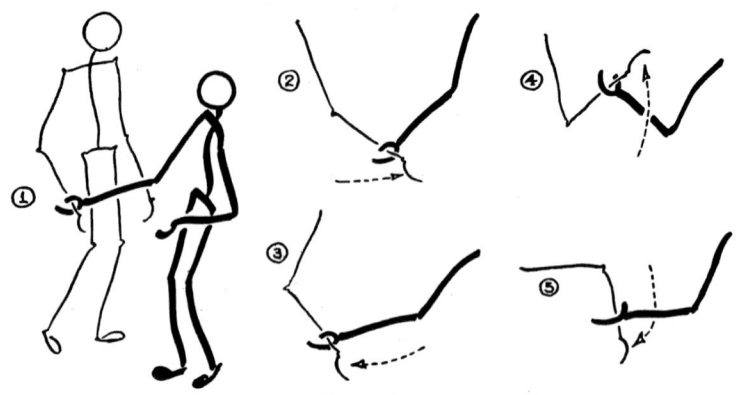

Fig. 208
Escape From Grip On Wrist
1.—He grabs *down* on your right wrist with his right hand.
2.—Swing your hand down to your left, against his fingers, until he resists.
3.—Then swing your wrist to your right.
4.—Then twist your wrist OVER his wrist to your left.
5.—Raise your right elbow up, twisting your wrist down AGAINST his thumb and out of his grip.

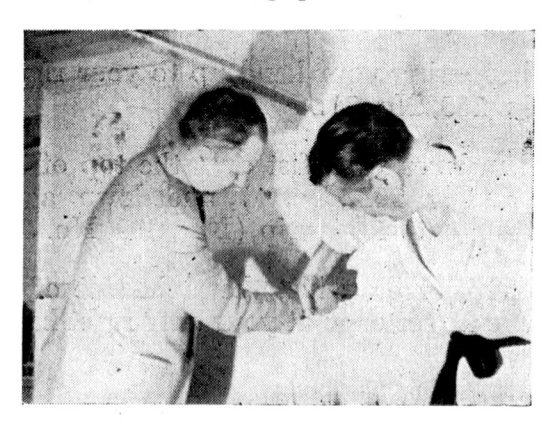

Fig. 209
He has grabbed down on your right wrist with his right hand. Swing your wrist to your left against his fingers, preferably until he resists and tries to pull your wrist to your right.

DEFENCE-OFFENSE MOVEMENTS AGAINST A GRIP ON YOUR WRIST

Fig. 210

Suddenly let your wrist go to your right, yielding to his pull, but going farther to your right than he anticipated.

Then lever your fist over the top of his wrist to your left, against his thumb, RAISING YOUR RIGHT ELBOW and pushing down with your hand, getting out of his grip.

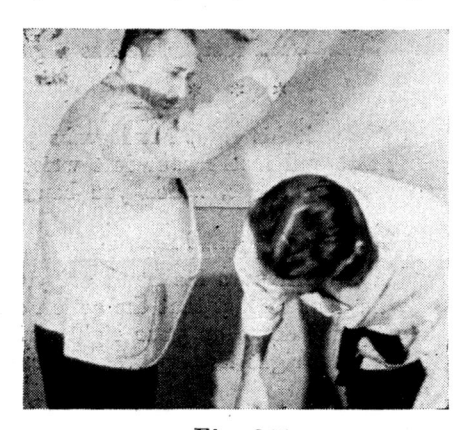

Fig. 211

Then strike the right side of his neck with the little finger edge of your right hand, if you get the chance.

OTHER METHODS

There are many other simple tricks which you may use to get out of a grip on your wrist. Want to know some?

● The Elbow Blow: If a man grabs your right wrist tightly with his right hand, or in civilian life, if someone tries to crush your hand in a handshake, reach *over* his right arm with your left arm and with your left hand grab down on your own right wrist near your hand and attempt to push it down towards the floor, as though you were trying to push your hand out of his grasp. Now here's the trick.

Inconspicuously aim your left elbow up at his jaw, then suddenly let go with your left hand and hit up under his jaw with the back of your left elbow. Make it a serial. Follow up with an edge-hand blow to his neck then a right knee to his crotch and then a right toe kick to his right shin. Frequently an adaption of the "Assault Trip Throw" will work in here.

* * *

● Another defence against a man grabbing *down* on your right wrist with his right hand is to swing your left hand over his right forearm, then under his right wrist and then slide it over the top of your right wrist. Turn his palm up and with your left hand lever your right wrist down out of his grip. Always try to go against his thumb. Always follow up with blows. Whenever you are using two hands against his one, work fast, as he has a free hand.

* * *

● Still another defence if his right hand grabs your right wrist is to close your left fist and insert your left wrist down deep in the angle between your right fist, which you bend back, and his right wrist.

Raise your right elbow and lever your right fist down against your left wrist which in turn prys his hand off your right wrist.

This can easily be done so fast that the action cannot be seen.

If his left hand grabs down on your right wrist, lower your right elbow and twist your right fist up over to your left and employ the same principle.

If he grabs *up* at your wrist, the method works just the same.

* * *

● Another point in passing. *"When he grabs, strike!"* Give him a hard edge-hand blow over the top of his forearm at the junction

DEFENCE-OFFENSE MOVEMENTS
AGAINST A GRIP ON YOUR WRIST

of about the upper and lower two thirds, over the region of the posterior interroseous nerve and brachio-radialis muscle. This blow may have a slight paralyzing effect and enable you to pull out of his grip.

DEFENCE-OFFENSE WITH BLOWS AGAINST A GRIP ON YOUR WRIST

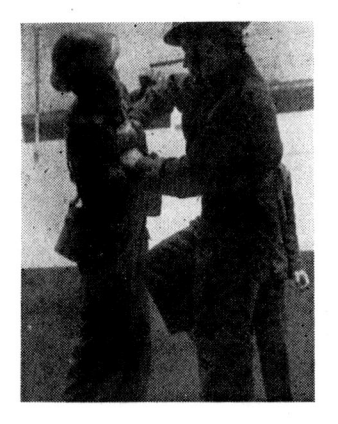

Fig. 212

What's happened? The soldier on the left has grabbed your right wrist with his right hand.

What about your fighting reflexes? What have you done?

Your left hand has grabbed down on his right wrist and pulled it down. Your right knee has come up to his crotch.

Now you are swinging your right elbow up across the front of his face, levering your right hand over his right wrist out of his grip.

244   ARWROLOGY

Fig. 213

Next swing your right elbow over his right shoulder, and smash it back against the right side of his neck (Carotid Sinus). Pull him into the blow with your left hand.

Fig. 214

Follow up with a back edge-hand blow against the right side of his neck.

(What if you get tangled up with his arms? Spin around to your right, moving into him, leading with blows.)

DEFENCE-OFFENSE MOVEMENTS AGAINST A GRIP ON YOUR WRIST

A complete series of Defence-Offense movements against one or two men grabbing one or both of your wrists from in front or behind, with one or both hands is fully described in Volume II.

ADDITIONAL NOTES FROM INSTRUCTOR ON CHAPTER 3.

Chapter 4

SEVERAL SIMPLE TRICKS

These simple tricks are inserted as aids only and are not to be considered reliable methods in their own right. But sometime they may help you to secure a more deadly hold. Remember that you should always try to end up with a deadly blow or death-dealing Arwr lock on your enemy, no matter how you start.

No. 1
Bend Back Finger

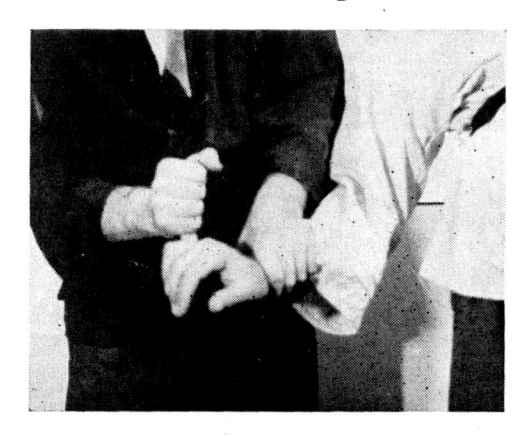

Fig. 215

A simple little trick which often helps to remove a man's hand from your throat or wrist is to grab one of his fingers, especially the little finger, and bend it back. This is especially effective if you hold his wrist firmly with your other hand. It's a fair grip to lead some men away with too.

No. 2
Push In Knee

Fig. 216

When behind a tall opponent, you may pull him down to your height by grasping his upper arms and turning slightly to your left, shove your right foot into the back of his left knee.

Then you may clamp a death-dealing Posterior Arwr Lock on his neck.

No. 3
Head Twist

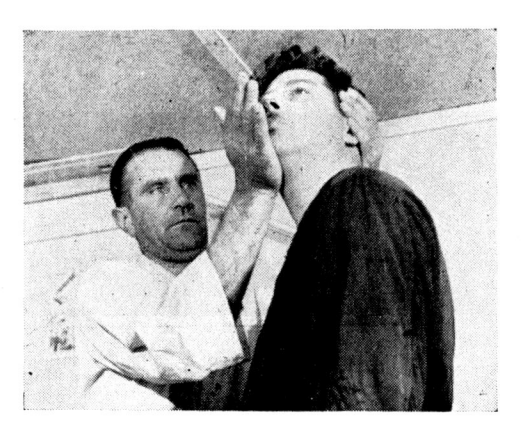

Fig. 217

Here's an effective little trick. Facing your opponent, your left hand goes over his right shoulder and grabs the left side of the back of his head. Your fingers go a little over his ears. Pull his head to your left.

The palm of your right hand shoves the right side of his chin to your right.

Thus twist his head around and clamp a death-dealing Posterior Arwr lock on his neck.

(His arms will not be by his sides as shown above. Catch on? Work fast! This trick has several applications, such as pulling a man out of a car.)

No. 4
Foot Twist

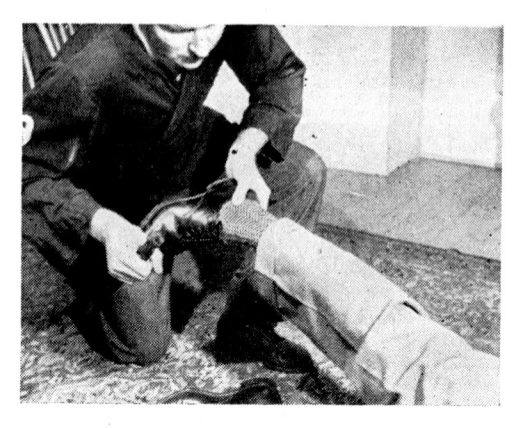

Fig. 218

Twist his foot to turn him on his face.

Sometimes it is advisable after throwing your enemy to turn him over onto his stomach. The reason is obvious, as then he cannot reach up at you and he has difficulty in seeing what you are doing.

With your enemy on his back, you have grabbed his right foot, heel in your left hand and toe and dagger in your right hand, and you have twisted his foot around so he is forced to turn on his stomach.

> Then you can spring on top of his back with the point of your dagger leading the way. Throw all your weight behind the dagger.
>
> If unarmed, jump onto his back and secure a death-dealing Posterior Arwr Lock on his neck. Remember it? You may also grip him tightly with your legs about his waist in the common "Scissors" hold, used so often in wrestling.
>
> Look out for kicks and bending of knees. Work fast.

SEVERAL SIMPLE TRICKS

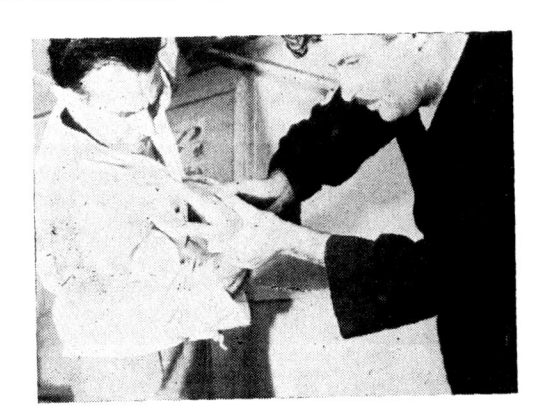

No. 5
Wrist Bend

Fig. 219

Instructions :

The Wrist Bend hold occasionally may be used to some effect.

First, with your left hand grab down on the thumb edge of his right wrist, so your thumb crosses over the middle of the back of his hand.

Bend his wrist in on his forearm, twisting his hand up to your left.

Second, your right hand reinforces the grip by grabbing the little finger edge of his hand so your fingers curl into his palm and your thumb crosses over your left thumb.

Bend his wrist in and twist his hand a little over to your left. Get in close and lever his hand down, probably bringing him to his knees.

> Look out for a blow from his left hand. Keep your right elbow and arm ready to guard your face. Work in close to your opponent in all these methods. Don't forget you've got knees to strike with, and so has he. Keep your right knee ready to deliver a blow, or to swing across to your left to guard your crotch. Turn a little left too, against knee blows.

No. 6
An Empty Gun Used As A Weapon

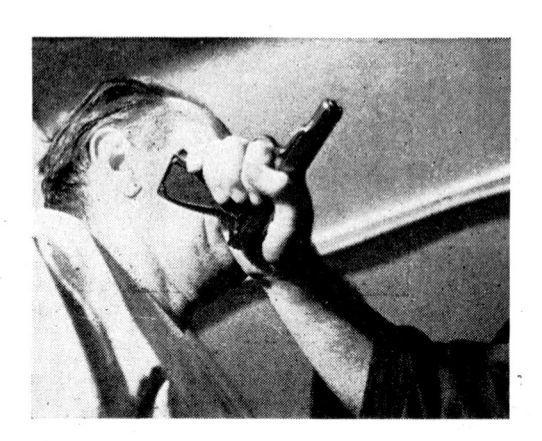

Fig. 220

After accurately emptying your revolver or automatic, grab the gun firmly as shown above, with your forefinger still over the trigger. You have flipped the gun back in your hand so your thumb grabs over the middle of the barrel and your fingers press up towards your index finger.

(If the gun is loaded this prevents the trigger being pulled in case you wish to give a blow with the gun when silence is preferred.)

The end of the butt juts out past the little finger edge of your hand. Now you can deliver the usual back edge-hand blows with the steel end of the butt.

Remember that the carotid sinus is a good spot to strike at in the side of the neck. This method keeps the gun more securely in your grasp than just grabbing the barrel. You can give more varied and more deadly blows with it, being able to strike *under* a helmet.

SEVERAL SIMPLE TRICKS

No. 7
Push In Knee

Fig. 221

If someone puts an arm lock on you, as shown above, a simple escape may be affected by turning sideways, and shoving in the back of your captor's knee with your foot, pulling out of his grip.

No. 8
"Spin Under" Escape From Arm-Lock

Figs 222 — 223

If anyone twists your left arm behind your back (Fig. 222), an effective defence-offense throw may be carried out.

It is an example of how the various methods may be applied to varying circumstances.

When your left arm is twisted behind your back, 1. Bend down low. 2. Duck around to your left, under his left arm. 3. *At the same time,* put your right leg behind his legs. 4. Slide your right arm across the front of his body, and throw him back over your right leg. (Right Assault Trip Throw, See Part II, Chapter 1.)

If he twists your *right* arm behind your back, bend down *low,* and duck around to your *right* so you face the same direction as your opponent. Put your left arm across the front of his stomach and put your left leg behind him. Throw him back over it (Fig. 223).

This throw should be performed so fast that no one should be able to see what actually is happening.

POINTS TO REMEMBER

1.—If anyone can see what you're doing, you're not doing it fast enough. (Or it's not dark enough.)
2.—If he grabs with both hands, strike.
3.—Watch what he's not using and what you're not using.
4.—Follow up when he's down.
5.—Standing throw, lying strike.
6.—When in a fight, spin to your right.
7.—Read, study, visualize, attempt, perfect!
8.—When you see a leg between your legs, pick it up.
9.—Do unto others as they would do to you, but do it first.
10.—Whenever your enemy grabs your wrist when you are holding a dagger, pull BACK and DOWN.
11.—It is difficult to duck under a man's arm.
   He can suddenly bend his arm and clamp it close to his body.
12.—To prevent a man from twisting your wrist, clench your fist tightly and straighten out your arm, forcing it down.
13.—When tying a man's wrists together be sure that
   (a) His fingers are out straight,
   (b) You tie *between* his wrists after tying about them.

WHAT ABOUT YOUR WEIGHT?

In training to become a Jiu-Jitsu expert, centuries ago, undergoing a diet for periods of about a month was considered important.

For those students who are not fortunate enough to be under the nutrition care of the armed forces, and who have no pathological condition present causing their abnormality of weight, the following diet suggestions may be of some value. Naturally they are not to be followed interminably.

For good general health, a sufficiently high vitamin and mineral intake must be maintained continually, regardless of any diet, and strict dieting should not be indulged in unless recommended by your physician.

However some men are obviously overweight or underweight simply because of poor eating habits.

HOW TO GAIN WEIGHT
Follow This Diet

Breakfast
    Cereal and plenty of cream
    Glass of milk
    One egg
    Bacon (1 oz.)
    Banana or prunes
    Glass of orange juice
    Three slices of bread and butter
    Two large tablespoonfuls of jam or jelly
    Eight teaspoonfuls of sugar and a cup of coffee!

At 10 *A.M.*
    1½ glasses of milk with 1 egg and cream
    (Chocolate milk if desired)

Lunch
> Serving of meat, chicken or fish (¼ lb.)
> Potatoes, spaghetti or rice (¼ lb.)
> Salad (Fruit 15% and lettuce, ¼ lb.)
>   (Mayonnaise)
> Two slices of bread and butter, or rolls
> Vegetables 3% (¼ lb.)
> Dessert (Pie, ice cream, pudding. ¼ lb.)

At 4 *P.M.*
> 1½ glasses of milk with 1 egg and cream

Dinner.
> Meat ¼ lb. (Or 3 eggs, 2 oz. cheese or 3 slices of French toast with 2 eggs)
> Potato, rice or creamed vegetable (¼ lb.)
> Two slices of bread and butter
> Vegetables 6% (¼ lb.)
> Dessert (As above)

At 10 *P.M.*
> Vegetables for sandwich (¼ lb.)
> Two slices of bread and butter.
> Glass of milk
> (Or large bar of candy).

Total calories approximately 5000

HOW TO LOOSE WEIGHT
Follow This Diet

Breakfast
> Four teaspoonsfuls of cottage cheese
> Half a slice of bread
> Half a cup of skimmed milk
> Tea or coffee. (If you can get it.)

Lunch
    Meat 1½ oz.
    One serving of vegetable 3%
    ¼ cup of skimmed milk
    One serving of fruit 6%
    Tea or coffee.

Dinner
    Three teaspoonfuls of cottage cheese
    One serving of vegetable 3%
    Half a slice of bread
    ¼ cup of skimmed milk
    Tea or coffee.

Total calories approximately 350.

SUBSTITUTES

Vegetables 3%

Asparagus
Beet greens
Cabbage
Cauliflower
Celery
Cucumbers
Egg plant
Lettuce
Mushrooms
Sour pickles
Radishes
Rhubarb
Sauerkraut

Spinach
String beans (Canned)
Squash
Tomatoes

Vegetables 6%

Beets
Carrots
Dandelion greens
Onions
Pumpkin
String beans
Squash
Turnips

Fruit 6%
Blackberries
Cranberries
Gooseberries
Lemons
Muskmelons
Oranges
Peaches
Pineapple
Strawberries
Tangerines
Watermelon

Fruit 15%
Apples
Blueberries
Cherries
Grapes
Huckleberries
Pears
Plums
Raspberries.

ADDITIONAL NOTES

R-OLOGY

The most difficult thing about Arwrology is pronouncing it. It is pronounced Ar-roor-ology. It means the science of All-Out Hand-To-Hand Fighting. It is derived from the old Welsh word Arwr, meaning a Hero, an All-Out Hand-To-Hand Fighter who wins.

For simplicity, the abbreviated form of R-OLOGY may be used.

ACKNOWLEDGMENT

Appreciation is given to the following for their inspiration and assistance in producing this book: Professor C. P. Martin, M.A., M.B., Sc.D., (Dublin), Robert Reford Professor of Anatomy, and Chairman of the Department of Anatomy, Histology and Embryology of McGill University.
Professor Fraser B. Gurd, B.A., M.D., C.M., F.R.C.S. (C.), F.A.C.S., Department of Surgery, McGill University. Associate Professor Chester E. Kellogg, B.A., (Bowdoin), M.A., Ph.D., (Harvard), Department of Psychology, McGill University.—Honourary Associates of the Society of Arwrologists.

* * *

John F. Davis, B.Eng., (National Research Council, Ottawa.) James Jorissen, G. R. Benskin, Geoffrey Hess, B.A., (R.C.A.F.)—Fellows of the Society of Arwrologists.

* * *

George Vickerson, B.Eng., Member of the Society of Arwrologists. G. Warren Brown, Associate of the Society of Arwrologists. H. R. Perrigard, A.R.C.A., Dr. D. McLaren, Clarence Dwyer and many others.

"Don't be an armchair Arwrologist—Try it out!"